# Bronsdon Ghosts and Mary McDonough

# Bronsdon Ghosts and Mary McDonough

*John Paul Rau Jr.*

ISBN-13: 9781546665526
ISBN-10: 1546665528
Library of Congress Control Number: 2017907811
CreateSpace Independent Publishing Platform
North Charleston, South Carolina

*Dreams and memories go hand in hand with thoughts that may have crossed paths with reality, or was it actually a dream? Everyone likely dreams, though some may not remember or may think of them, as Ebenezer Scrooge did, as "a bit of bad meat. Humbug!"*

*Then there may be others who remember a bit but quickly forget. The brain works in mysterious ways and functions while your body rests. Some may awaken from a dream confused but unshaken. Others can become quite rattled by their dreams.*

*Logically, if these dreams happen when we're asleep, without knowledge of why, then simple intelligence should be able to experience them when we're awake as well.*

*Not everyone has daydreams; most people are so active that any dreams are totally missed. I dream quite often, day and night, asleep or awake, because I am looking forward to them, as my dreams are my memories and my reality.*

*My great-aunt Mary McDonough had the ability to dream of her memories, of which she had many, and then to speak of them as they were relived in her mind. This book is dedicated to Aunt Mamie and Jack McDonough.*

# Contents

# Acknowledgments

—⌒—

THIS IS AN INTERESTING PART of writing a book. Something that started out as memories with stories from my great-great-aunt, my grandmother's aunt. Having a very old book on family history was a tremendous motivation. This made me feel as though it had been waiting years to be further researched and retold.

Computers started evolving into mainstream use for me in 2000, and then the web became available. This was a beginning that would open doors to the past and help preserve some rich history of times gone by.

You may have heard or even said "the good ol' days." When things were easy and life was simple, even before cars.

The Bronsdon family, as it was, made a very important impression on me from an early age. Knowing all my grandparents to some degree and hearing about their pasts gave me my own impression and thoughts about their personalities.

Letters, newspaper articles, deeds, and wills—she saved them and passed them along to me. Much information was gained from this material about events so long ago. I have come to realize that she saved all the things she considered precious to give to me, so I could tell Mamie's stories, add pictures and they would become timeless one day.

I want to thank my friend Dana Csakany for helping with my pictures to make them usable for print. Every picture used on the interior Dana cleaned, changed to black and white and increased the resolution to meet the print specification for publishing. Dana lives in Eugene, Oregon and works in the print industry.

Mary Catherine McDonough 1900
Mamie

# CHAPTER 1

# Dreams May Come True

THIS NEW WORLD MAY HAVE been discovered by Christopher Columbus in 1492 or the Vikings long before that. Many touched these shores and found them very much inhabited, but not by white men. The Pilgrims came in 1620; we know that too from our history and heritage. Many of the descendants of the ship bearing the name *Mayflower*, which carried 102 passengers and thirty crewmen, populated the country and the world with lengthy lineage connections.

There are many crossing paths among our ancestors. These passages I have written concern many Old and New World experiences throughout my own family's existence in this country and abroad, over decades, years, and even centuries. My late family members had very fruitful, some colorful, and most very fulfilling lives during trying times in this early American colony and country. I have been gathering information for many years; in fact, I now realize that I've been storing some of this mentally without even knowing why. I have always wanted to write something, mainly for the creativity and learning experience. Similar to woodworking, using your mind and hands can be relaxing.

Knowing myself, I need a purpose to act on any project; there has to be an objective. I have sat many times with paper and pencil or pen and later a computer to more easily try writing some words, but it is something that cannot be forced. Eventually, I became resigned to my not being a writer, as this is not a talent of mine. Then one day in mid-April, just before Patriots' Day, I remember, I had an inspiration that started to consume my thoughts, and I began to write. The words came and seemed to just flow at times, like someone was using my fingers to type his or her will. Thoughts were coming to me as clearly as if I had been there myself, or maybe I had. My daughter Kerry Ann was an inspiration after I started this, as she is very passionate about her spirit life.

Using Ancestry.com and having my DNA done added much more information and then brought together many people and dates that made my work more productive.

Quite valuable to my research was the *Bronsdon and Box Families* history, a book written and published by another ancestor, Mrs. Harriet F. Parker, in 1902. I have an original copy that my mother gave me back around 1995. I studied that book for twenty years prior to my writing. This historical knowledge and other information led me to Milton Cemetery, knowing that I have a son buried there with my grandmother, Avis D. Rau.

There were days when I was working on the road as a salesman that I would stop there and have lunch while reading the Bronsdon book and wondering about history before computers. It's a very quiet and beautiful place to visit. Mrs. Parker lovingly and painstakingly put the book together for her husband, William Creighton Parker.

One man with tremendous knowledge of the Bronsdon family ancestry was Colonel Lucius Bolles Marsh, who was born in Danvers, Massachusetts, on April 18, 1818, the son of Captain Thomas Hartshorne Marsh and Sarah Curtis Bronsdon Marsh. The Marsh family name dates back to Salem in 1633 and then to Plymouth and the *Mayflower* in 1620. The colonel was a very intelligent man and learned to read by the age of four.

In 1895, while living in retirement in North Scituate, Massachusetts, Mr. Parker, Harriet's husband, came to visit Colonel Marsh with hopes of obtaining information about their family. The colonel was the oldest living Bronsdon descendant, and Mr. Parker knew he was an active genealogist. During his research, the colonel received some family history by chance, and it would contribute a very interesting discovery to their book and to ours.

William Parker was a Bronsdon descendant through his mother, Margaret. She was the daughter of Phinehas Bronsdon, a man with a great family and personal history. The colonel contributed what verbal history he thought important directly to Mrs. Parker. But as he was aging and wanted to clean up his desk, he relinquished all his history to Mrs. Parker. With this information, the Parkers, along with William's mother, then living with her son as she was in failing health, sorted and arranged their book to get it published. On April 25, 1902, the first edition was stamped by the Library of Congress.

Colonel Marsh died while proofreading the book on August 14, 1901, at his home in North Scituate, never getting to see the final work. There was help from other family members, including financing the publication by paying the print cost for individual sections of the book.

Milton H. Bronsdon became responsible for the early history in England. He hired and paid Mr. Lothrop Withington, a very highly regarded genealogist of the time, and with this information, what had been stories and traditions were now researched and written facts.

Lothrop Withington was born in Newburyport, Massachusetts, on January 31, 1856. He was noted for his work on the history of the Revolutionary War and passenger ship manifests during the Great Migration. While returning from England on May 7, 1915, he was killed in the sinking of the RMS *Lusitania* after it was torpedoed by a German U-boat.

I am also in possession of an antique black doctor's-style instrument bag filled with papers, letters, coins, stamps, and pictures by Mamie (Mary) McDonough. She had left this with my mother to give to me one day. This brought more insight into much of my family members' past. The bag sat in my house for many years as time went by, until thoughts about my past surfaced again. I was sitting in my kitchen trying to figure out how to remaster and frame a picture of Jack McDonough that showed him buying his garden seed on March 1, 1957, in Boston. It's actually a section from a newspaper, and there is a caption below Jack's picture that reads, "John McDonough of Readville, who has had his own vegetable garden for years will be at it again this spring. Now 80 years old, McDonough drops into a downtown Boston store to make his selection of seeds. Jack told the cameraman, 'I dig up the garden myself.'" The picture shows a tall, thin man, well dressed in gray wool suit, vest, and tie, with a handkerchief in his breast pocket, a black fedora, polished black shoes, and a wooden cane. An overcoat is draped over his left arm—dapper. He has seed packets in hand and is selecting more.

That day, April 17, was when I had an inspiration. Once I decided to start writing about my thoughts and dreams, the next thing I knew, there were ten pages, and the number was growing.

With a mixture of names, dates, facts, thoughts, and maybe some speculation or dreams, I can sit in a quiet place and hear Mamie talking. She would just go on and on as if in her mind, she was right back in her own story.

Here is *my* story through Mamie's rose colored driving glasses

## CHAPTER 2

# Early History

*There were four knocks upon my cellar door,*
*Though no one there, of this I am sure.*
*The dogs heard it too, and they were right here.*
*They barked and they barked as though they could hear.*
*I checked outside to find no one there.*
*What made the sound is not at all clear.*
*It felt quite strange and should fill me with fear,*
*But if there was a ghost, it didn't appear,*
*Though it did make me feel that someone was near.*
*It now makes me wonder if Henry McDonough is here.*
*Next day I began to write with great flair*
*I have his journal and handle with care*
*Henry long dead, many a moon has since passed*
*Now the memory of Mary McDonough will last.*

THERE IS ONE THING THAT will never change and no one can alter: the spirit of your family. They were here and made your history. Some good, some maybe not. Some left fingerprints and footprints; others left facts and figures, books, pictures, and stories.

Without stories we would not have an intelligent reason to wonder who our ancestors were or how they have affected our lives today. I am very thankful to be writing these passages, happy to know that my descendants will be able to trace their history of emigrants, Native Americans, and the people who helped shape this country as we know it from the earliest of times.

These are the ghosts and spirits of our past.

*He who loses money loses much, He who loses a friend loses more, and He who loses his spirit loses all.*

—HENRY MCDONOUGH, 1948 (WHO *IS* HENRY?)

Our story begins in England in 1638 with the birth of Robert Bronsdon, my seventh great-grandfather. Born to a family with means to afford him an education, he would take his young wisdom and explore a new land. The first known record of Robert Bronsdon's being in Boston is a marriage certificate that marked the first of his three marriages in New England.

That first marriage of Robert Bronsdon, merchant of Boston, was to Bathsheba Richards of Lynn on April 15, 1667. She was born about 1647 in Massachusetts and died in Boston in 1678. It is thought that she had been quite sick and was expected to die, as Robert remarried quickly. There is little record of the second marriage to Rebeckah Cooley in January 1678. She was born in Boston in 1640 and died in 1689 while living in Boston. Robert Bronsdon's third marriage was to Hannah Breeme on April 12, 1694. She was born on June 12, 1668, and died in 1730 while living in the North End of Boston. This was recorded in the books of the Olde North Meeting House by Reverend Cotton Mather.

Cotton Mather was born in 1663 in Boston, which was then part of the Colony of Massachusetts, to parents Maria Cotton and Reverend Increase Mather, a prominent Puritan minister who was a pastor but very much involved in Boston politics. Having attended Boston Latin School and Harvard College, Cotton Mather graduated in 1678 at age fifteen. He lived on Hanover Street from 1688 to 1718, was influential in the moralities of his time, and was supportive of the Salem witch trials. He died February 13, 1728, and is buried in the Mather tomb at Copp's Hill Cemetery on Hull Street in the North End of Boston.

Boston is named for the largest borough in the town of Lincolnshire, England. One notable structure there is Saint Botolph's Church. During the early 1600s, this borough was alive with religious contempt. In 1612 Vicar John Cotton, with his radical preaching, was responsible for the increase in church attendance. He would be a catalyst in telling people who wanted more religious freedom to join the Massachusetts Bay Company. Some did join, sailing to New England and helping create the village of Boston in 1630.

John Cotton was born in England in 1585 and married his first wife, Elizabeth Horrocks, in 1613. They had no children. She died in 1630.

John Cotton would emigrate in 1633.

John then married Sarah Hankredge Story, daughter of Anthony Hankredge and widow of Roland Story, they had emigrated in 1632 and settled in New England.

John and Sarah had six children, including daughter Maria Cotton, who was born in 1642.

John Cotton died in 1652.

Richard Mather, born in England in 1596, first married Kathrine Holt in 1624. They had a son named Increase Mather, born in 1639 in Boston. Kathrine died in 1655. Richard married Sarah Cotton in 1656. This marriage made Increase Mather and Maria Cotton stepbrother and stepsister. They, too, were married in 1661 and had a son named Cotton Mather in 1663.

Lineal descendants bear the same surname and blood of an ancestor and are direct descendants. Indirect descendants are of the blood but have a different surname. I am one of Robert Bronsdon's many indirect descendants.

I feel that Robert Bronsdon and his lineal descendants need to be highlighted on their own, as they add to the rich history of this family. The fact is that if Robert hadn't traveled to the New World to find his place, my entire history would have been very different.

To show some perspective, in what would be New England and Boston but was the village of Boston in the early 1670s, there were but a dozen merchants.

There was a time about 1635 when Dorchester went from the Neponset River near Milton to Narragansett Bay off what is now Rhode Island.

Ships were moored in a rudimentary harbor; goods were floated out and loaded for distant ports. Quality lumber was cut from the huge pine, oak, maple, and birch trees that surrounded the village. This resource was helping build the village of Boston. Lumber was valuable for trade, and shipping loads to the South Atlantic and Caribbean brought a tidy profit.

Boston Harbor 1670

This meant men were needed for labor. Finding a growing village with bountiful resources, men flocked to this lucrative place to settle, bringing families, friends, and religious groups.

At this time the area was still very much inhabited by Native Americans of various clans. There were village camps with small huts and longhouses that were commonly used by large clans. They would be seen regularly in the harbor, fishing the huge weirs that were full of bounty. Lobsters were so abundant that the natives would pluck them from the sea by hand. They would light a fire in a big pit, add rocks to heat up, and then lay seaweed over the superheated stones. Lobsters would be piled on the seaweed and then covered with more seaweed, hot rocks, and huge sheets of tree bark. Sand was placed on top to help seal in the heat, and as the lobsters steamed, the entire area smelled wonderful. Clams, oysters, and fish were added as well.

The area was also abundant with game such as deer, ducks, turkey, and geese. There seemed plenty for all.

Robert Bronsdon was a prominent merchant and became known as honest and fair. An association of men in the late seventeenth century built wharves for the shipping trade and houses for the multitude of people who were finding work in lumber. Some men became farmers to support the need for food, others were fishermen, and everyone needed shoes with the village growing. Mr. Bronsdon made good on everything he did, from buying land to building housing and wharves. His favorite houses were in rows along the harbor, where he would receive rent for the wharf and warehouse use. Housing space could be anything from a room for a sailor to a house for a family. He bought as much land as he could and had the finances to mortgage a property as needed.

The leading merchants of Boston built their wharves one hundred yards offshore so they could claim the area in between as theirs. Eventually, they added pilings to extend the land out into the harbor. Houses—big, beautiful homes for the wealthier families and sea captains—were built on the waterfront, notably in the North End of what was now a growing Boston.

With the population rapidly increasing, Robert could afford to buy ships and trade goods in the markets of the West Indies, Caribbean Islands, and Cuba for sugarcane, while trading lumber that had been cut from land he owned rather than being brokered creating larger profits. He was able to have men producing lumber from his tree lots along the Massachusetts coast up into what is now Maine. It was then loaded onto his own ships, cutting out the middlemen. When the men cut wood and cleared a lot, the trees were replaced with a structure. Houses and warehouses were being built at a steady pace.

The lumber that was shipped was sold before arrival. Loads of sugarcane coming back to him for making rum were like gold. Robert would get top dollar upon delivery, and everyone profited.

One such venture was shipping wine from Madeira, Portugal. It had to be transported in hot, humid conditions for months. This young wine did not keep well. They found that adding a stronger alcohol called *aguardiente* to the wine to fortify it made the nectar age very nicely in the same ships and conditions. It became the preferred beverage of the time—Madeira wine.

The English were determined to control all trade in the colonies, and in 1651 Parliament passed the Navigation Act. This forbade the colonies from trading with anyone other than England.

The merchant ship *The Pink Lady*, owned by Robert Bronsdon and a partner, Mr. Russell, and mastered by Captain William Blake, was directed to be put ashore for inspection on April 18, 1689. The ship was laden with 148 barrels of Madeira in the hold. In 1682 Mr. Bronsdon had been one of several businessmen to petition His Majesty's officers for grievances associated with customs charges. On this day in 1689, Robert knew the revenue officer very well, and a bribe was easily conveyed. His ship was allowed to sail on to a port with no revenue inspection. The inspector was supposed to send these taxes back to England, but Robert knew the revenue officer pocketed the money. The bribe left Robert in control of the amount he paid, and he might need to use this man for future shipments.

Robert Bronsdon had eight children, all born in the North End of Boston. By 1689 he had accumulated much wealth, including a wharf, fifty vessels, thirty houses, some livestock, and one Negro. He died November 22, 1701, leaving many worldly possessions. After his death, his last will and testament was read on October 23, 1702, by Samuel Greenwood, his son-in-law and a prominent man in Boston.

Though there are many descendants of our great ancestors, having healthy children was difficult.

The first of Robert's children born were to Bathsheba. Mary, born on September 22, 1668, died as an infant. She was twin to Elizabeth, who would marry Samuel Greenwood. Elizabeth died December 9, 1721.

A second daughter named Mary was born on August 27, 1670. She was married to Captain Jonathan Evans. Mary died September 5, 1737.

The fourth child and first son, Joseph, was born on August 7, 1672. He died in 1697 at age twenty-five, leaving a widow, Dinah, in Lynn, Massachusetts. Following the very difficult birth of Joseph in 1672, Bathsheba became quite sick and never really recovered. She died sometime around 1678.

After the death of Bathsheba, Robert married Rebekah Hett Cooley on January 3, 1678. She was born in 1640, in Lynn, Massachusetts. Her father was a prominent businessman in the area. She and Robert had four children. Their first child, Rebekah, died at birth October 7, 1679. Second was Sarah, who was born in 1682. She married William Clark and died in 1762 in Boston.

One thing Robert always wanted down deep was to name a son after himself. Robert Bronsdon II was born on July 28, 1684, but sadly died October 13, 1695, at only eleven years old.

Robert's only surviving son was Benjamin, born on August 30, 1686, to Robert's second wife, Rebekah. Benjamin, at only fifteen years old, was Robert's oldest living male heir upon his death in 1701. William Clark, who married Robert's daughter Sarah, was chosen by Benjamin to be his guardian. He was afforded the means to be properly educated and well dressed. At age twenty-one, he joined the Second Church, where he had been baptized as an infant.

Benjamin, my sixth great-grandfather, was married to Mary Bant on March 25, 1707, by Reverend Increase Mather in Boston. Mary was born in the south end of Boston on March 22, 1691, the daughter of Captain Gilbert Bant, one of the wealthier men in Boston. She became quite ill in early 1751, and Benjamin married his second wife, Elizabeth, before Mary died on October 6, 1751.

Altogether, Benjamin had seventeen children, many of who died young.

Benjamin and Elizabeth took up residence at the Bronsdon mansion, located along the northern battery. Adjacent to and across from their residence was the Bronsdon section of the wharf with warehouse and brewhouse. Benjamin owned more warehouses along Merchants Row, as well a major section of the outer wharf that his father had built.

Benjamin Bronsdon was now a wealthy merchant of Boston. After becoming a sea captain, he made more land purchases. Tragically, on April 12, 1757, Benjamin died unexpectedly at seventy-one. He is buried at Copp's Hill Burial Ground, old ground, tomb number one. Benjamin had the tomb built about 1717 in the oldest part of the cemetery. Tomb 119 was Robert Bronsdon's original location in 1701. The entrance to the tomb is identified by a stone curb inscribed "Bronsdon" on Hull Street in the North End. The entrance is below ground now, but the inscription can still be seen from inside the cemetery today.

There is another inscription on the tomb that was presented by the Bronsdon heirs upon the death of Elizabeth in 1810, as she was Robert's last surviving grandchild. It reads, "This tomb belongs to the heirs of Miss Elizabeth Bronsdon who departed this life March 20, 1810 at age eighty-two."

The oldest surviving son of Benjamin Sr. was Benjamin Bronsdon Jr., born in Boston on February 28, 1715. He inherited considerable wealth from his mother's family, the Bants. He then became a mariner, which makes the history of his early years, including his first marriage, difficult to address. There is a record of his second marriage, to Elizabeth Foxcroft, on January 4, 1750. She was the daughter of Judge Francis Foxcroft of Cambridge.

Many records of the time were lost to fire with the approach of the Revolutionary War.

Benjamin became a member of the Freemasons of America in 1741 and eventually traveled to England, staying there and making that his home.

Benjamin Sr. had a second surviving son named Bant, my fifth great-grandfather, born in Boston on October 23, 1721. His mother was Mary Bant. Bant married Elizabeth Box in 1750. She was born in Boston on Cambridge Street in a house where the Revere House is now situated.

Captain Bant Bronsdon

Like his older brother, Benjamin, Bant was a mariner and was away quite often. He had seven children with Elizabeth. Captain Bronsdon died somewhere far from home around 1765, leaving Elizabeth a widow until her death around 1790.

Bant Bronsdon's fourth child, a son named Benjamin, was born in Boston on October 23, 1757. He married Salley Kneeland of Roxbury, who was born in 1759. Captain Benjamin Bronsdon was the militia captain of Milton Company.

As was common at the time, all boys without a father would learn a trade. John Box Bronsdon became a boot maker; Bant a baker and rope maker; Benjamin a butcher and market merchant; and the youngest, William, a sailor. They were all worthy trades of the day and occupations that made money.

John was a private in Captain Josiah Vose's Milton Company, which was part of the defense of Boston's coast from April 13 to April 26, 1776. He was also assigned to Lemuel Robinson's regiment in Concord with Captain John Bradley's company. This man was a true New England patriot of the American Revolution.

John Box Bronsdon, my fourth great-grandfather, was the first of the family's fourth generation. He was born on May 21, 1751, the son of Bant Bronsdon and Elizabeth (Box) Bronsdon. He was named after his grandfather John Box and was born on land that is now part of the Old State House property but belonged at the time to John Box, rope maker. John Box Bronsdon married Abigail Baker of Stoughton on August 9, 1774, at the age of twenty-three. He had acquired land and built their house in Milton. The farm and orchards he developed produced an abundance of cherries from trees that lasted more than two generations. They would have cherry blossom festivals in early May and harvest festivals in the summer. Farming became more than just growing produce for his own family, as he soon found out how well his crops grew. The Blue Hills would change the wind and weather, creating good growing conditions. The soil was deep and rich because of the natural slope that let minerals and water run off the hillside, and there was irrigation year round from springs that left running brooks of cold, clear water.

Sarah Curtis Bronsdon was the fifth child of John Box Bronsdon and Abigail Baker. She was born on February 24, 1783, in Milton, Massachusetts.

Sarah married Captain Thomas Hartshorn Marsh on November 29, 1814. Thomas was the father of Colonel Lucius Marsh, who obtained some interesting information during his research. He acquired papers prepared by Edmund Baker regarding Richard Baker dating back to 1635 in Dorchester. These papers showed his lineal descent from Mrs. John Box Bronsdon or Abigail Baker; she was a daughter of Elijah Baker and Hannah Puffer. This was the same Baker lineage that would one day see Walter Baker taking over the chocolate business from his father. Under Walter's guidance, the business started to prosper in 1824.

Being the son of a prominent military captain, Lucius Marsh was inspired by his family's past. Captain Marsh's grandfather Captain Thomas Hartshorn was in the Eighth Massachusetts Company under the command of Colonel Michael Jackson and remained active until peacetime. Lucius's father, Captain Thomas Hartshorn Marsh, received his commission during the War of 1812 and commanded a militia company trained as minutemen. He lived with his son the captain into his old age, dying in Fairfield, Maine, on September 15, 1822, at the age of eighty-three.

John Box Bronsdon gave his service to the patriotic cause and in 1776 helped defeat the British and establish American independence. From Massachusetts archives, we find John included in muster roll calls. He is recorded in Captain John Bradlee's militia company with Colonel Lemuel Robinson's regiment on December 21, 1775, defending the town of Concord for seventeen days. Again we find him with Captain Bradlee on March 4, 1776, helping erect a fort at Dorchester Heights for five days. Some two thousand patriots erected that fort under the command of General George Washington. Using their own oxen, they led some three hundred teams with wagons, delivering material to Dorchester in the dark of night while muffling the noise of the wagons and chains. Trees for the fortification had been cut and hidden on the Sumner Farm in Milton about ten miles from the Heights. The men worked through the night with barely a word spoken, and by first light it was evident that they had built an impressive shield. Massive cannons were moved there from Fort Ticonderoga in New York.

Flag of America's original thirteen colonies 1776

British General Howe's first reaction was to attack, but a massive snow-storm changed his decision, and on March 17, 1776, with eight thousand men and ships, the British sailed out of Boston Harbor to Halifax, Nova Scotia. General Howe was the officer who'd had the North Church torn down for firewood in 1775. Originally built in 1649 in the North Square of Boston, it was burned down in 1676 and rebuilt the next year.

After the revolution John Bronsdon's real estate holdings increased dramatically in and around Milton. It was the English way to own as much land as possible. After his wife, Abigail, inherited real estate from her grandfather in Randolph, Mr. Bronsdon bought up all other shares, ending up with twenty-five acres.

The Bronsdons named their first son Phinehas. He was born on May 7, 1775, and died at only thirteen months old on June 22, 1776. They had another son on April 6, 1790, and again named him Phinehas. He was my third great-grandfather, and he was also born in Milton. He married Rachael

(Marston) Lee of Gloucester and had eight children. Phinehas died December 28, 1861, and Rachael on July 1, 1872. They are buried in Milton Cemetery.

John and Abby's second surviving son, Benjamin, was born on July 1, 1778. He married Nancy Wade Damon in July 1805. She was born in Scituate, Massachusetts, on May 4, 1780, to Zadock and Thankful (Wade) Damon. Benjamin died suddenly on July 18, 1832. Nancy died February 6, 1862. They are buried in Milton Cemetery.

John Bronsdon was born in Milton on April 9, 1798, to John Box Bronsdon and Abigail Baker. He married Elizabeth Holmes of Stoughton on July 6, 1814. Elizabeth was the daughter of Samuel and Rachael Holmes. She was born on December 4, 1788. John died in an accident on February 15, 1832, and his widow died October 5, 1846.

James Edverdus Bronsdon, my second great-grandfather, was born in Milton to Phinehas and Rachael on July 5, 1818. He married Delia E. Sanborn on October 6, 1866. Delia was born in Maine on August 23, 1843, to William Sanborn and his wife, known only by her family's name, Murch. Delia died May 3, 1879. James died January 8, 1899. They had two children: William Cushman Bronsdon, my great-grandfather, born on July 14, 1868, and Murch Marston Bronsdon, born on May 18, 1870.

There are many more spirits of the past that should and will be recognized, but for now I think we need some substance of how this family continued to evolve and prosper from their time in England through Puritan times and colonial New England and into the nineteenth and twentieth centuries.

This first ancestor, Robert Bronsdon, is responsible for many people and events that shaped countless lives, and a lot of this rich history took place right on the edge of Boston, Massachusetts.

CHAPTER 3

# Readville

CAMP MEIGS, ON A SECTION of land adjacent to Boston, is the former American Civil War training camp that existed from 1861 to 1865 in Readville, Massachusetts. It was connected by rail line and was called a *cantonment*, which was a Swiss army term describing a permanent military station as opposed to a temporary field camp.

This was where the first official African American unit in the United States, the Fifty-Fourth Regiment, trained. By the spring of 1863, the Boston black community was fully behind the regiment. Men were coming from afar to sign on. They would be trained by Captain Robert Gould Shaw of the Second Massachusetts Infantry. He was made colonel of the Fifty-Fourth upon arriving in Boston on February 15, 1863, to assume his duty and train his men. By May 14, 1863, the Fifty-Fourth was fully staffed at more than one thousand strong, all proud to serve their country during the Civil War. This regiment helped establish significant patriotism, and the decision was made to establish the Fifty-Fifth in Readville as well.

The camp ran from Sprague Pond on the northwest end to the Neponset River on the southeast. It was established on twenty-four acres that had been used in the past for militia training and now, in 1861, two temporary encampments. Over the next year, the permanent camp was built. It was called Camp Meigs, after Quartermaster General Montgomery Meigs.

Ebenezer Paul owned the entire area at the time, and when he discovered that soldiers were using the land, he protested. The war department then began paying him $300 a year for its use.

After the war ended, Meigs was abandoned, and the entire farm was sold to Charles A. White of Hyde Park for $20,000, including structures and equipment—anything that was left. Mr. White divided the land into sections and eventually sold it all to private parties. Some of that land was also traded for labor when money was too scarce for payment. This included the meadow area near the river that was prone to flooding.

During the time the military camp was active, there were wooden barracks that could be seen across the plain from the pine-covered slopes of Blue Hill.

View of barracks at Camp Meigs from Blue Hill

The parade grounds were in central Readville, with an impressive display of cannons. In 1869 the Norfolk Agricultural Association acquired a portion of the parade grounds, improved upon it, and ultimately, it became the Readville Race Track.

In 1890 the Hamilton Park Association was organized, and in 1894 its name was changed to the Meigs Memorial Association. Several years later, on January 4, 1903, the name of Hamilton Park was changed to Meigs Memorial Park.

Today, Readville is a section of the Hyde Park neighborhood in the city of Boston.

It was called Low Plains from 1655 until 1847, at which time it was renamed for Mr. James Read, a resident and cotton mill owner.

This was actually part of Dedham until 1867.

The Readville rail station has a long and rich history in early train transport. In 1876, just over ten years after the end of the war, the area became a junction for trains coming to and leaving the Northeast; they went through Readville Station.

Readville, Massachusetts 1876

This was also the intersection of the Blue Hill Station that ran a trolley up to Blue Hill Avenue, stopping in Milton at the foot of Blue Hill where there was an attended station with heat in cold weather. From this location, horse-drawn trolleys went to Brockton and beyond.

It would be a useful location for future growth. The area was bordered by the town of Milton to the south and the town of Dedham to the southwest.

Dedham is the location of the first man-made canal in North America. Called Mother Brook, it joined the Charles River with the Neponset. The altitude difference created a strong current to turn several mills downstream, creating industry and jobs.

The Fairbanks House in Dedham is recorded as the oldest surviving timber structure in North America, having been built about 1637 for Johnathan and Grace Fairbanks. They lived there with their six children, as many generations of descendants did later.

Fisher Ames, an American patriot, was born in Dedham on April 9, 1758. He began studying Latin at age six and entered Harvard at twelve, graduating in 1774. He then began teaching, and he was admitted to the Massachusetts bar in 1781 and the Massachusetts House of Representatives in 1788, taking part in ratifying the original US Constitution. Ames was later elected to the First US Congress, defeating Samuel Adams.

Paul's Bridge, Readville, Massachusetts

The bridge is a stone structure providing access over the Neponset River. Crossing over the bridge is Milton Street, the border of the town of Milton, which is just on the other side approaching from Readville. This is one of the oldest bridges in Massachusetts. It was built in 1849 by Thomas Hollis Jr. of Milton, replacing the earlier Hubbard's Bridge built before 1759.

The name Paul can be attributed to the owner of the adjacent land on the Readville side with views of great Blue Hill. The area was inhabited by a large population of the Massachuset Indian tribe. The wetlands area known as Fowl Meadow borders the river and is rich with fish and wildlife.

Traveling a short distance along Milton Street, one comes to the village area and train station.

Blue Hill Community Church was founded in 1888 and located at the corner of Milton Street (now Neponset Valley Parkway) and Hamilton Street leading into Wolcott Square. Reverend Phillips Brooks preached his last sermon here, and his Christmas carol, "O Little Town of Bethlehem," had its first performance in this quaint place. Samuel Francis Smith first read the second stanza of his poem "America" at this tiny church in Readville prior to its reading at the Washington Celebration of 1889. In later years it was put to music, becoming a classic patriotic song, also known as "My Country, 'Tis of Thee." Smith died suddenly while traveling by train to Readville to preach at the church. He is buried in Newton Cemetery.

The city of Boston established itself as the transportation hub of the Northeast with its network of railroads and proximity to a good harbor for international trade. Just as important were the intellectual, educational, and medical opportunities in the nineteenth century. The city was dominated by an elite known as the *Boston Brahmins*, and they flourished. Culturally, they became renowned for literary composition and lavish artistic patronage as writers, historians, theologians, and philosophers. The term *Boston Brahmin* was coined by Oliver Wendell Holmes Sr. to classify the oldest and wealthiest New England families with English heritage. They paved the way to building what would someday become a world-class city.

There was another advantage to being in Readville, away from the urban density of the city with its crowded tenements and trash. In times past, hygiene went from rudimentary to nonexistent. There is a belief that body odor and poor dental health was so widespread that everyone had a stench, and so no one thought or wrote about this. Most times, daily washing meant only hands and face. Twigs of herbs and pine branches were used indoors to help with odors. Going for a swim was also an opportunity for cleansing. Sprague Pond, being spring fed and very deep, made for a great place to swim in the summer.

There was a story told, which I heard from my father, about a circus train arriving in Boston. Something happened, and the train rolled over into the pond and disappeared, never to be found. Whether it was the depth of the pond or the mud and silt at the bottom, the story scared me enough to keep me from ever swimming there.

Back before the mills and factories generated pollution, the Neponset River was another good place to spend a hot afternoon jumping off Paul's Bridge into clear, cool water.

# CHAPTER 4

# The Hickeys

IN 1872 A YOUNG IRISH immigrant by the name of James Hickey, a farmer, settled in Milton and became a US citizen on November 4 of the same year. He was married to Bridget McDermott and had a daughter, Annie Josephine Hickey, in 1871.

This was the start of a whole new and exciting life in a new and fertile country.

Annie would one day become my great-grandmother.

Bridget McDermott was born in 1838 in County Cork, Ireland. She was the daughter of Timothy McDermott and Ann Travers. Bridget arrived in America sometime around 1865.

James and Bridget's family consisted of six children. The oldest son, James, was born in 1866. John born in 1868, Annie in 1871, Timothy in 1873, and Frank in 1875. Little is known of the four brothers within the history that I have recorded. Later, on February 8, 1878, another daughter, Mary Catherine Hickey, was born.

Boston was a haven for Irish immigrants following the potato famine in Ireland during the mid-1800s. The old colonial New England Yankees hired Irish as laborers and servants; they were thought of as a lower class. When the War Between the States erupted in 1861, many Irish immigrants joined the army to fight for the North. This show of patriotism began to change the way Yankees felt about the Irish.

James Hickey was born in County Limerick, Ireland, on August 28, 1837, and baptized at Saint John's in Limerick City by his parents, Patrick and

Maria Hickey. Although he was naturalized in 1872, James actually arrived in New York City on May 16, 1863. He found refuge from the flourishing and at times hectic city environment in the small town of Milton, where he labored and raised livestock and, along with his wife, Bridget, a family. Life was all about home, and in the dense quiet of the town, it was very peaceful.

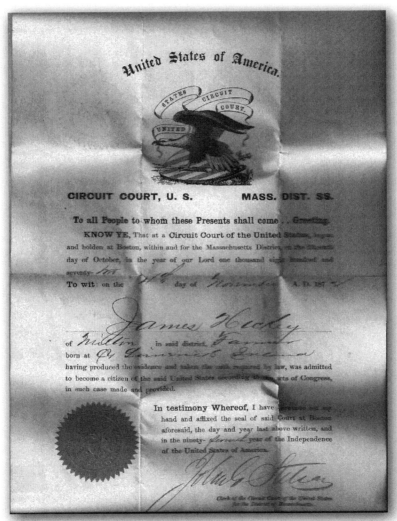

Naturalized in 1872

With four sons and two daughters, living space was tight, though young men would find their own places in the world. Annie, the oldest girl, grew up learning domestic skills, which were all very important at the time. This would entail feeding livestock, harvesting and preserving food, and cleaning properly to avoid illness. Cooking on a wood stove challenged many learning cooks. Annie was known and well-liked by the many acquaintances and friends she enjoyed visiting.

Annie Josephine was actually the second Annie born to the Hickeys. Two years before, they'd had another daughter named Annie. She died within her first year.

Mary, being seven years younger than Annie, learned much from her sibling, but Mary had a way with life on the farm. Her mother had been trained to work with horses back in Ireland, and now she would show her daughter. Mary loved being with the livestock. Feeding and caring for them came naturally to her, and she became a great help to James after his sons began moving on to their own lives.

Life progressed in the quiet town of Milton, and going to nearby Readville, with its railyard, shops, and post office, was as good as going to the big city. The post office was on the main road, which was Milton Street, across Hamilton Street was Blue Hill Community Church. This area would become much more as the region grew.

CHAPTER 5

# Ghosts of the Great Blue Hill

JAMES EDVERDUS BRONSDON, BORN IN Milton on July 5, 1818, was the first son of the sixth generation of this Bronsdon family. He married Delia E. Sanborn on October 9, 1866. She was born in Maine on August 23, 1843, to William Sanborn and Matilda Murch.

James and Delia would be my second great-grandparents.

Delia died May 3, 1879, and James died at age eighty on January 8, 1899, while living with his son William C. Bronsdon. He was a skillful hunter and guide, which he passed on to his sons. They are buried in the family plot at Milton Cemetery.

James's father, Phinehas Bronsdon, born in 1790, was an inventive, mechanical man. He became an apprentice, learning all aspects of ironworking and blacksmithing. After seven years as an apprentice, Phinehas built a shop of his own and hired men to work for him. He became well known in his trade, and men would travel many miles for employment. The shop was on his own property on Canton Avenue in Milton, a fine location, having seven stagecoaches on his route. He served as farrier to all the horses and made repairs to the coaches and wagons as well. Roads were terribly rutted and bumpy early on, and the shop was always busy repairing broken wheels and axles.

Phinehas, being strong and athletic, could swing a sledgehammer in both hands simultaneously with ease. He could run like the wind and was quite proud of his power. Like many of the time, he enjoyed hunting in the Blue Hills, and he quickly became aware that there were deadly dangers. The area was infested with rattlesnakes. While Phinehas was apprenticing, he made himself a pair of iron tongs to capture the snakes. When he was on his hunts and spotted one, Phinehas would run to capture it by the head with his tongs before the snake could coil. He then killed it and cut off the head. He had learned that the detached head could still bite and cause serious injury, if not death. Phinehas would take his snakes and hang them from a nail at his shop, and with a tool he developed, he peeled the skin right off clean. Then, hanging in the hot air by his forge, the skins dried out nicely.

One day, a passenger on a hackney coach saw some snakeskins hanging and inquired if they might be for sale. Being a hatter and leather man, he was interested in decorating his wares with the contrasting skins. The men made a deal, and Phinehas found a new way to make money while enjoying himself.

The snakes were quite evident in other incidents near the property on Canton Avenue.

William Bant Bronsdon, a baker, was the twelfth child of John Box Bronsdon. Born in Milton on September 21, 1798, he married Elizabeth Bowman on November 27, 1825. Elizabeth was born on June 16, 1803, to James and Susana (Hunt) Bowman of Milton.

William's bakery was on Randolph Avenue, not far from home. He was noted for his corn bread. People came from all over. During blueberry season on Blue Hill, he would employ many pickers, bartering blueberry corn muffins in trade.

Elizabeth was at home one day watching her daughter Abigail playing in the front yard and noticed her sitting still, staring at a stick. Then she saw that the "stick" had a waving head on the other side of a small log. Now realizing it was a rattlesnake, Elizabeth calmly coaxed Abigail away slowly until, at a safe distance, she swept her up and took her into the house.

Another time at the bakery, a rattlesnake fell from the wood pile, causing much scrambling until William killed it with a club.

Phinehas Bronsdon Jr., born on March 5, 1822, in Milton, married Sarah King Loud of *Mayflower* ancestry. She was born in Pittston, Maine, on January 28, 1828. They were married in Boston by Reverend Sebastian Streeter on October 17, 1847. Reverend Streeter, a Universalist minister, married many of the time and was noted for marrying 118 couples in 1843 alone.

Phinehas Jr. became a city forester in Boston at twenty-two years old. The mechanical skills he learned while working for his father afforded him the ability to study engineering. Around 1857 he was involved with constructing the first horse-powered railway in the country, which went from Boston to Charlestown. Then in 1859 Phinehas moved his family to San Francisco.

This was a milestone in Bronsdon history, as it had now been nearly 200 years since Robert Bronsdon came to Boston. Phinehas was Robert's first lineal descendant to reach the Pacific coast.

In San Francisco Phinehas built the first street railway on the hills, known as the Omnibus, as well as railways in Portland, Oregon, and Los Angeles, California, later becoming superintendent of street railways. His son continued his father's work, becoming a rail constructing engineer at age twenty-one and building railway systems across the country. In 1898 he built an incline railway in Saint Paul, Minnesota. He later organized the Providence Association of Mechanical Engineers, becoming its president in 1901. He was a thirty-second-degree Freemason and a member of the organization established in England in 1717 as the Grand Premiere Lodge of England.

Having members of the lodge in England becoming established in Boston, member Henry Price was picked to go and petition in 1721 for a warrant to establish a lodge in Massachusetts. In 1733, Henry Price was given his warrant with lodge creating him as the Provincial Grand Master of New England. The Grand Lodge of the Most Ancient and Honorable Society of Free and Accepted Masons of the Commonwealth of Massachusetts now known as Saint John's Lodge. The lodge appointed in 1746, John Box, Master of the Lodge, in 1751 my fourth great-grandfather John Box Bronsdon would be born and named after his grandfather. John Box was also Warden of Kings Chapel and the Vestry, he died October 21, 1774 aged 75 years.

Phinehas Sr. had seven children, his fourth being a daughter, Margaret Matilda Bronsdon, born on January 11, 1824, in Milton. She married Creighton Whitmore Parker Sr., born on Fort Hill, Boston, on March 10, 1824. They were married by Reverend Edward Beecher in Boston on April 4, 1848, and resided for many years at 28 Lowell Street, Lynn, Massachusetts.

They had three children born in Boston, including one son, Creighton Whitmore Parker Jr., born on October 23, 1854. This man deserves credit for inquiring about the Bronsdon ancestry around the turn of the century. He knew that Colonel Lucius Bolles Marsh was one of the oldest surviving members of the family and had a genealogy background. He would eventually contribute much research and facts to print.

Sometime during the late 1800s, Colonel Marsh came upon some important history written by Edmund J. Baker, the original chocolatier. Born on April 20, 1770, he moved to Dorchester Lower Mills and became the proprietor with water rights on the Dorchester side of the Neponset River in 1791.

The writings that Marsh came upon concerned Richard Baker of Dorchester, 1635. This included information about Mr. Marsh's maternal grandmother, Mrs. John Box Bronsdon or Abagail Baker.

He also found documents from John Box, maternal grandfather of John Box Bronsdon, shedding light on additional ancestry knowledge not previously known. Upon Creighton's inquiry to Colonel Marsh, it was discovered that while the Parkers were tracing the Bronsdon history, Colonel Marsh was accumulating piles of old records to relate this history for future generations.

Harriet F. Parker 1900

The Marsh genealogy and the Bronsdon and Box history were collected into a book copyrighted in 1902 by Mrs. Harriet F. Parker of Lynn, Massachusetts. That book has been very helpful with early history.

James and Delia had two children, William Cushman, born on July 14, 1868, and Murch Marston, born on May 18, 1870. The brothers ran the established freight and livery business with offices at 67 Franklin Street and 15 Merchants Row. While running a depot carriage business from William's home at 19 Hamilton Street in Readville, Murch lived in a house in Milton built by his great-grandfather in 1774.

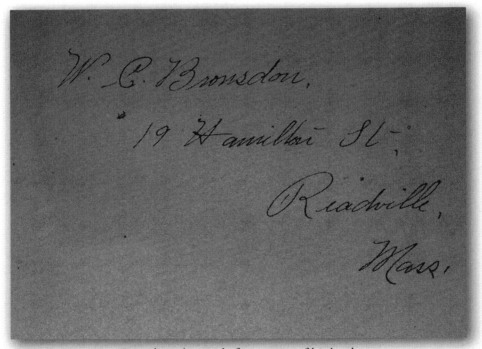

Signed on the inside front cover of his book

I have had my great-grandfather William Cushman Bronsdon's copy of the 1902 book for many years and have studied it many times over. This was another inspiration to continue this history, as it relates to so many of my ancestors, the information they left, and a lifetime of experiences of mine—places

I have been to and stories that were told that relate to the Bronsdon ancestry and my life. Knowing some of this rich history and adding to this knowledge is gratifying. But much more important is putting these words into print and sharing them with generations to come. I fear that without this, part of my family legacy would be lost forever.

Great Blue Hill rises to 635 feet in Norfolk County, situated in the towns of Milton, Canton, and Randolph, Massachusetts. The state name is derived from four Wampanoag words used by the Massachuset clan of natives who lived on the hill and around this area: *massa*, meaning *large*; *adchu*, meaning *hill*; *es*, meaning *small*; and *et*, meaning *place*. Ten miles from downtown Boston, it can be seen from Boston Harbor and for ten miles or more in all other directions. It looks out over Readville, Canton, Milton, Dedham, Stoughton, and Randolph, and that is just to the northwest. Moving to the other side of "Big Blue," one can see Quincy, Braintree, and downtown Boston. Six thousand acres became the protected area known as the Blue Hill Reservation.

The year was 1814, and an industrious young man by the name of James Read built a massive textile mill, calling it Dedham Manufacturing Company. The structure was the second in size only to Slatter's Mill in Rhode Island. He brought on such great prosperity that it became known as Readville Cotton Mill, and the area around it was called Readville.

Many of these industrial mill buildings still stand, with the railroad tracks on one side and the river on the other. Central Park Avenue (Hyde Park Avenue today) ran between them, flanked by buildings. The railroad was in back of the structures, traveling parallel to the avenue.

With its location adjacent to Boston and growing business economy, Readville made a good place to run a livery business.

# CHAPTER 6

# Bronsdon Express

Bronsdon Badge

WILLIAM AND MURCH BRONSDON WERE brothers, business partners, and friends. Brought up in Milton learning the horse and carriage business from family, they would inherit office and warehouse space in downtown Boston from their uncle, and together they would acquire property with a barn in Readville. They established an express office, Bronsdon Brothers Express, with a livery service on Hamilton Street feeding, grooming, and housing horses for hackney carriage service as well as moving and delivering freight. William, or Billy as he was called, and his brother Murch helped care for the horses and all other aspects of running a livery business in the somewhat-established town of Hyde Park.

The firehouse in Readville was all horse driven at that time. Billy and Murch cared for some of the horses that were not on duty at nearby station, next to the Sprague Street Bridge, as there was little stable space. A team of four of horses were at the station as long as there was someone on duty. Otherwise, the horses were close by at the brothers' yard. The station house had a bell tower that rang loud and clear when a team was needed. Eventually, they cared for the horses at the Engine Four Firehouse on Blue Hill Avenue in Milton as well, along with the new firehouse right at the corner of Hamilton Street in 1918. The Boston Fire Department still houses *Engine 49* at 209 Neponset Valley Parkway today.

The men were moving freight all around Boston and running the carriage service through the surrounding towns to the train depot in Readville. Business was good. Billy had been able to acquire wagons and various tools from Mr. White when he was selling off Camp Meigs after the war. Many things were just left behind.

The brothers cleaned and repaired a house on the lot adjacent to it at 19 Hamilton Street. It had been military housing at one time. Billy lived in the house, and they ran their business from there. Murch was living in the Milton house he had built on the old Bronsdon land originally purchased by his great-grandfather John Box Bronsdon in 1774.

On February 27, 1895, Murch married Emma Louise Fredricks. She was born on February 15, 1876, in Milton.

Emma's father, William Augustus Fredricks, was born in Boston in 1835. William Fredricks married Cristina Rosina Hauser in 1872. Cristina was born in Württemberg, Germany, on August 27, 1847, and came to America the same year, departing from London, England, and arriving in New York. It is not known if Cristina changed the spelling of her name; it may have been done at the immigration office. Her birth record from Germany lists her as Christine Rosine Haeusser. Her parents were Bernhard Haeusser and Eva Marie Fischer.

One sunny early spring day in late March 1895, Annie was at the Readville post office sending out letters. Upon leaving she noticed a handsome young man walking toward Hamilton Street. Just then, there were fire bells started ringing. Men came through Wolcott Square on the fire wagon and took off up the Milton Street toward Paul's Bridge, bells ringing. Once the commotion was over, the man, now watching the firemen turned to continue on then stopped when he noticed Annie watching him and tipped his hat in acknowledgment. He then turned around and walked over to the post office. Stopping in front of Annie, he introduced himself.

"Good day, miss. My name is Billy Bronsdon."

She introduced herself, and Billy asked if he could walk her back to her carriage where her father was to meet her. Billy waited until her father returned. When James did return, Billy introduced himself as William Bronsdon, and James introduced himself as well and added that he had heard that the Bronsdon boys were fine young men.

This was the beginning of a new life for Billy, twenty-eight, and Annie, twenty-five. They would see each other many times over the following months. On Christmas Eve 1895, Billy asked Annie to marry him, and without hesitation, they were wed on January 15, 1896.

They lived in the house on Hamilton Street and had three children: William Cushman Jr., Avis Delia (she would be my grandmother one day), and John Paul, who was called Jackie.

The house and livery office was just the right size while the children were small, and they had most everything that was needed. But as the world moved ahead toward a new century, Billy was thinking about more space. Moving anywhere was out of the question. This was their life, and it was very good there.

The livery office was in the rear of the house across from the barn that went back another thirty feet and a corral off to the left. Just inside the door of the livery office was Billy's desk, a big rolltop with many compartments. Each box belonged to a customer, service, train car, or other order that required Billy to have a carriage or delivery wagon available for service at short notice. The boxes in his desk carried names that had levels of response, because if William Bronsdon told you he would be there, come hell or high water, it would be done. Billy personally saw to certain customers. Reputation was very important for the business.

Billy was not big into smoking, just an occasional cigar, but he did keep a pipe and tobacco pouch at the desk "for times I wanted to think," he'd say.

There was a table always set up and ready for a game of checkers or chess in a corner, and a dartboard hung above the table. Billy had a drifter friend—a hobo, but still a friend—by the name of Ralph. His looks could almost pass for white, but he could have been a Negro or an Indian even. He could throw a dart exactly where he intended darn near every time. This was impressive to watch, and Billy enjoyed throwing darts with him, watching every move and trying to figure out how he could do this. He never did figure it out.

On December 16, 1912, while attempting to jump on an outbound train, Ralph slipped and was killed by the train. Billy had him buried properly and paid the expenses. It bothered him badly for a period of time.

Murch liked to play chess, but he couldn't find many who were even reasonably suitable opponents. Murch did not like to lose. Billy got used to losing to him rather than having Murch not talk to him for the day. After losing, Murch would just chew on an unlit cigar and stew at his desk. The cigars were gone, so it was assumed he ate them.

No one ever asked.

Situated in the back of the freight office was Murch's desk, another roll-top, but smaller, as he liked to keep his figures to himself. He was responsible for paying bills and the employees' wages. Murch had a similar mailbox-type cabinet by his desk that was used for finished work needing to be billed.

Right in the middle of the office was a big round cast-iron coal stove. During the winter it would be roaring with heat. On a stand adjacent to the stove was a coffee pot that always had some good, strong coffee ready. This was Billy's first stop in cold weather. He would shake down the coal grate from the previous night's stoking and open the draft and flue. That gave him time to run to the outhouse while the coals got nice and red again, and then he'd add chunks of coal, depending on the day's weather. During the winter he would put twenty-five pounds of coal in at night and set the flue and draft low, and that would burn all night and heat all the way through into the house. The doorway to the house led directly into the kitchen with its wood-burning cookstove at the back wall that pretty much kept the rest of the house warm. Billy had made a grate that fit the kitchen cookstove so they could use coal, but their food didn't taste at all the same, so they would just use wood. That would have been the only difference in the cooking of food in Billy's lifetime, being before gas or electric.

The front of the house had a dining area and parlor with a small stove that helped when it was extremely cold. Billy would heat up a large piece of coal in the office and bring it out in a metal ash bucket just to take the chill off at times.

One of the best parts about this fuel was that the Bronsdon Brothers were in the coal business, too.

Coal had been used for thousands of years but was not available in America until around 1750. The cost of shipping it from England was too high, and only wealthy families could afford it, but with wood being readily available, it wasn't necessary. By mid-1800, a new industry was underway, and canals were dug farther inland, making waterways for moving material to access points for further shipment. Barges pulled by mules were used to haul the coal down the canals.

Early steam engine trains were soon burning coal. They could get more power from the heat of coal, and the trains ran more efficiently. This cut down on fuel cost, and the fire tender had an easier job. From the late 1800s to the early 1900s, all steam engines on trains, on ships, and in industry were using coal. This was to be the future of fuel, and as the railroads moved west, coal was fueling the move.

Readville was a hub for the time, having a train station and locomotive shop located adjacent to Wolcott Square. The railroad could take rail cars out of service for repair with the multiple tracks available. Trains that were on schedules were usually in by midnight. The yard crew would then take over moving train cars onto various tracks for further shipments.

There was a daily Readville freight car that had mail and packages for delivery in the area. This car would be moved to the station dock by 2:00 a.m. for the night clerk, Wendall, to sort out and get ready by 4:00 a.m. with slips into mailboxes and packages available for pickup.

The railroad station had an extensive freight board that covered incoming and outgoing trains. Times, freight on board or FOB, bills of lading, and schedules at the station would be on a chalkboard. Forwarding slips were placed in call boxes that were assigned to delivery companies. The delivery slips were picked up daily by Billy. They provided their services seven days a week. Sunday was just a little less busy than the average weekday. But they still had people who were driven to church and home and others needing transportation.

Readville Station had many society types from Milton who required service to and from the trains, and it paid very well.

From the railroad station, Billy would walk over to the little shop called Brewers Coffee House and have a cup of coffee while discussing the news of the day, if any. The shop wasn't named for the product they brewed. Leeds Brewer was the owner's name; he was from an old Yankee family in Hingham. Brewers had a wood stove just for roasting coffee beans and brewing good, fresh, hot coffee. The roasting beans smelled wonderful. There was an area set up for making donuts, which was Leeds's wife Charlotte's job. Donuts fried up fresh and hot with a good cup of coffee were all they sold, and they closed when they sold out for the day.

Leeds Brewer had an uncle who was a sea captain sailing the Caribbean Sea. Captain Charles Brewer delivered goods like lumber and other building material to the islands. One of his early voyages took him to the English island of Jamaica, where he was loaded up with goods to take back to New England. While waiting for his ship to be loaded, Captain Brewer was invited up to a plantation on one of the mountains. There he was served the best coffee he had ever tasted. Charles became friends with the plantation owner, and when he had the opportunity, he would bring home several bags of coffee for select friends and family. The rum he brought home was quite smooth as well.

Next to the shop was another freight office. While sipping his coffee, Billy was already directing two of his drivers as to what their day would bring. The morning ritual was all done on foot, as it was just a short walk, and he enjoyed the fresh early air.

William Bronsdon was not a big man, but he was a strong man. He was built like his grandfather Phinehas, who could swing sledgehammers with both hands at the same time. When Billy was working his horses, he seemed to be bigger than life. You would find him wearing his deerskin hat with the wide brim that a friend had made for him one Christmas several years before. Everyone, it seemed, knew Billy, and he was very good natured, willing to help out anywhere he could.

Once the day's duties were assigned, it was back to the livery. Stopping in the barn where the men were getting horses ready and loading deliveries, Billy would give a few directions and then write out the train schedule on the barn chalkboard before heading to his desk to finish sorting slips and planning. He always had the schedule up first thing, as any hoboes who might have spent the night were looking to see when their train was leaving and on what track. Billy didn't mind the men, and sometimes boys, checking the schedule since they did chores for him, and it was better that they be safe.

Murch would get in while Billy was still out, but his day had already begun before he got to Readville. He had his own routine as well, stopping at the firehouse up in Milton by Blue Hill on Atherton Street. Murch lived close by and stopped every morning for a cup of coffee with his friend and fishing partner, Patrick, who sounded like he was still in County Cork, Ireland. Patrick Michael Nee (or Paddy, as he was called) had been in the United States for twenty years but never lost his brogue. It was his duty to be at the Milton station overnight because there were horses that needed to be there in case of fire.

This station was different from the Readville station, where the Bronsdon livery was just five hundred feet away. From there he would go to the Blue Hill Post Office to pick up slips from Milton residents for deliveries or times to be picked up in a carriage.

Now Murch would light a cigar and head off to the freight office in Mattapan, then down to Cleary Square in Hyde Park, and to another stop down on Business Street between Hyde Park and Readville. There was a very busy freight office there because of all the factories and mills. Then on down to Readville, leaving his horse and wagon to the men, who would either prepare it to go out or unhitch the horse and put her in the corral area.

By the time Billy got to his desk, Murch had sorted and placed slips in all the compartments for Billy to work through and plan his routes. There were some trips that he made daily and others that were weekly. There were certain customers in Milton who, when they said 8:00 a.m., expected you to be right on time.

Once all his drivers were out, it was Billy who would make any special deliveries, ensuring no mistakes.

Billy and Murch had another office at 15 Merchants Row that had been in the Bronsdon family for many years. The family had owned this property all the way back to when it was waterfront right at the entrance to Long Wharf. One needed to cross the swinging bridge to get to the building. Then, as the harbor was filled in to increase the land mass, the wharf got shorter, and the water was farther from the office.

There were a tremendous number of goods coming into Boston by ship, and the Bronsdon's were positioned to get their portion of freight. The agent tending the office at Merchants Row was Billy's longtime friend Edward Martin, who was six years older than Billy. Edward's job was to peruse the offices along the wharf for future shipments, checking ship schedules. He was always up early as well, collecting slips at four freight offices and hand delivering them to a conductor on the first train heading to Readville every morning. The slips would most always be there for Billy when he made his rounds, but there were many situations of the day that could influence local events.

Wednesday was always an important day. There would be a wagon going to Faneuil Hall to pick up meat, cheese, and a few other perishable items. Wednesday falls in the middle of the week, and perishables needed to be kept cool. Storing food was just a normal part of life at the time. Many staples didn't need to be chilled but would be fine in just a cool or shaded area on the countertop. Eggs were stored on the counter in a wire basket for air circulation. They were mostly fresh daily but could stay there for a week. Cheese, butter, and milk needed to be chilled in the icebox, used pretty much daily. Between the city and Readville, just about all items were delivered to butcher shops and markets. After making his stops and finishing in Readville, he brought whatever was left on board back to the office.

Billy and his men usually ate steak on Wednesday nights.

There were dairy and sheep farms scattered all around, and many sold their stock as needed to make money to live on. There was a small slaughterhouse in Hyde Park that would take a cow in for slaughter and salt all the meat to preserve it without refrigeration in the winter. The salted cuts were corned and put into wooden casks rubbed with lard on the inside to make a good seal. This meat could be stored for use in the spring. Dried beef and jerky were readily available and were used for a common meal of creamed chipped beef on toasted bread, my father's favorite.

Ice was used for chilling meat, and that was not very efficient. In hot weather, butcher shops would bring in ice daily. Covering the ice with sawdust and burlap would help insulate and preserve it. Cold storage in winter made things much easier. The floors were all covered in sawdust as well; it absorbed water and any slippery bit of wayward meat scraps that the cat hadn't found.

Cats were a necessity for keeping vermin in control. Mice and rats were a constant problem, but a pair of cats living in the shops helped.

It wasn't until the late 1800s that ammonia was used to produce refrigeration with electricity. When the liquid is charged, it vaporizes into a cold gas, which flows through pipes to cool large insulated areas, creating refrigeration. This type of technology was slow to expand to ordinary citizens, but it was a boon for the meat industry.

Men had been trying with some success to ship meat on freight cars laden with huge blocks of ice. Some wealthy meat packers in Chicago devised a rail car just to accommodate the use of ice. In 1852 John Plankinton established a meat-packing house in Milwaukee called Layton and Plankinton. In 1863 Phillip Danforth Armour bought huge amounts of pork figuring the meat would sell for a premium price during war time, making him $2,000,000.00. His brother Herman then becoming a partner of Armour. The company expanded and opened branches in other cities and states including New York. Then in 1864, the brothers, led by Phillip partnered with John Plankinton established Plankinton & Armour Company. Both men experienced at distributing food across the country. After 20 years in partnership in 1884 the business ended. Armour continued with operations in Chicago, Kansas City and New York.

Good refrigeration was not yet widely available. In 1898, during the Spanish-American War, Armour sold the military half a million pounds of beef. Many men were becoming sick. The meat was tested, and more than 750 cases were rotted.

Hormel Foods, another big packinghouse in Chicago, was always trying to find ways of sending less scrap to the boneyard. In 1937 the company developed a process that removed all the meat and fat from the bones. They mixed it with flavor-enhancing spices and salt and packaged it in tin cans.

This was the creation of Spam.

This new product was shelf stable and could be shipped anywhere. It provided fatty calories that could be eaten anywhere, and it fed soldiers during World War II. Some loved it, many hated it, but they all ate it.

The Bronsdon boys did well and paid handsomely for hard work. They were known to be tough and at times overbearingly difficult, but they seemed to know what they wanted and paid nicely as well.

It was necessary for the Bronsdon's to have trustworthy men who could carry and use a sidearm. Many times, livery drivers would carry money, and there were road thieves lurking in the shadows. Billy always instructed his drivers to "hightail it out of there if possible"; otherwise, the men would have to depend on their own wits. The last thing Billy wanted was to have a man killed.

One fall evening, as Billy was coming in from Dedham, he encountered a young boy in a very dark area. The boy told Billy he wanted the horse and for him to get down and move away. Instead, Billy asked him, "Why?" and the boy stuttered that he needed to go. Billy kept talking to him and finally asked if he had eaten lately. The boy replied no. With that Billy told him to lower his hand—"I see you're armed"—and said that he would not give up the horse, but he would gladly give the boy a plate of food and a hayloft to sleep in for the night.

Billy reached out to shake the boy's hand and asked, "What's your name, son?"

"Fred. Fredrick Stewart."

"So what, now you want be like the outlaw Jesse James?"

Fred had traveled down the coast on a lumber train from Maine. Just outside Readville Station, he was spotted by railroad police and tossed off to the side of the tracks. That night was a turning point for this young man. He went home with Billy and ate dinner with a small group of hoboes who would be his bedmates.

Hay was important crop, and there were fields of it in Milton and Canton that needed to be cut, baled, and stored for year-round use. The horses depended on hay as fodder. The brothers had fields that had been in the family for years. Many were rented with the promise to supply the landowners with hay for their own use.

The Bronsdon's hauled hay to the train depot to be shipped to military bases. They had contracts like their uncles before them for hauling freight and stocking other goods, like firewood, coal, and lumber.

Billy didn't get involved in the haying work. The area over through Dedham and Milton had good hayfields, and the farmers hired labor as they needed it. The Bronsdons were hired to move the hay to the freight yard. The men working for Billy would set up wagons in the hayfields the day before it was to be loaded, and the hay crew would start as soon as they could see by daylight. If there was rain, the work was put off to let the hay dry; otherwise, the wet hay would rot. They used a baling machine from the late 1800s that made standard-size bales, but the men making them had to learn how much hay made a bale that was movable by one man. The early bales sometimes weighed three hundred pounds. The correct weight was between sixty and seventy-five pounds; the bales had to be thrown up onto a wagon, an almost impossible task if they were heavier. But another problem with heavy bales was the price. A farmer was paid per bale, not by weight.

Once the wagons were full, the Bronsdon's would move them to Readville Station in the late afternoon to be loaded onto train cars overnight.

Billy worked with a broker on large shipments, so he got a little less for the work, but he was paid when the hay was brought to the depot. The broker had to wait for the hay to be delivered to be paid.

# CHAPTER 7
# Mary Takes the Reins

Toward the end of 1899, Annie's sister Mary was not feeling well and seemed be sick all the time. She began losing a lot of weight, getting down to ninety pounds. At the age of only twenty-one, Mary was deemed hopelessly sick with lung problems, possibly tuberculosis. Her physician told her only continuous life in the open could help relieve her condition. She contemplated moving to Colorado, as many did at the time for clean, fresh air. Mary's next thought was the Readville racetrack and her love of horses; it was close to home and outdoors.

One of Mary's friends in Milton, Miss Brooks, who was an author, had relatives in England. She would get letters from her cousin Annie Fenn. They had been communicating since they met on a voyage to Kingston, Jamaica, in 1890. In 1891, Miss Fenn married Theodore Cockerell, a noted naturalist originally from London, where the air was much worse than it was in Boston. From 1890 to 1891, Theo was the curator of a museum in Jamaica, becoming a world-renowned professor of entomology.

In London in 1887, he and a school friend had contracted tuberculosis and needed better air quality. It was common to send someone to Colorado for its clean air and elevation, the thinking being that breathing the thin air was more difficult than breathing at sea level and would help strengthen the lungs. Theo was lucky to have a wealthy friend whose family paid the passage for both men, who sailed from England to New York, arriving in June 1887.

Theodore Dru Alison Cockerell would live in Colorado for three years, in small towns called West Cliffe and Silver Cliff in the Wet Mountain Valley.

These were booming mining towns at the foot of the Sangre de Christo Mountains. The name of the mountains is Spanish for *blood of Christ*. The sunrises and sunsets can evoke bloodlike colors in the sky.

Theo lived for a time at the Pines, a comfortable ranch about ten miles out of town. He left there in 1890, cured, and went back to London to marry Annie, with whom he had communicated with letters almost daily while in Colorado.

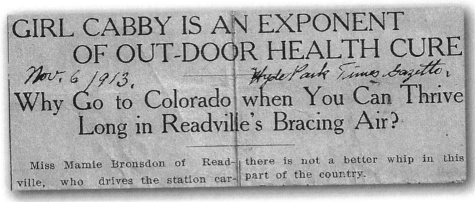

This made Mamie consider moving to get healthy, but the thought of leaving home made her stomach weak.

Boston was growing on the cusp of the twentieth century, and many of the wealthy businessmen of the day wanted what was now the city of Boston to become world class. The city was burgeoning with immigrants, and city neighborhoods became ethnic sections: Irish, Italian, German, Jewish, and more. The lowest class had the smallest population; strength was in numbers. There was no sanitation, and trash was everywhere. Growing pains, this was said to be.

If you left what is now downtown Boston and passed through Dorchester and Hyde Park down Central Park Avenue, as it was known in 1876, and the Neponset River with railroad tracks running parallel, then turned left under the arched granite tunnel that carried trains above at Readville Station, the area you reached was like not being in the city. It was still busy but much smaller and less ethnically diverse. There were fewer factories, and past the post office, the area was quite rural and unspoiled with woods and meadows.

Trees lined what few streets Readville had, and housing was not the brick tenements that lined city streets but wooden houses. These weren't elaborate, but most were neat and comfortable. Some of the residents made a habit of burning their trash in barrels outdoors. There were gardens on everyone's property, and some planted decorative flowers along streets and walkways.

Past the post office a mere half-mile along Milton Street was Paul's Bridge and the Milton town line. Milton Street began at the dam near the woolen mills on Mother Brook in East Dedham. Then the road went pretty much straight all the way to the bridge crossing Central Park Avenue just before the post office where the avenue continued to the Readville Race Track, with its grand stone entryway.

With fewer people and less housing and traffic, the air was much cleaner. Then leaving Readville toward Milton, the area became forested and very rural. The area covered by the Blue Hills was about six thousand acres of trees, meadows, ponds, and hills teeming with game and fish. There were the sounds of birds and clean air with no smoke. This was less than ten miles from downtown Boston.

Upon hearing about the situation, Billy Bronsdon, being Mary's brother-in-law, took it upon himself to offer to set her up with a horse and carriage, so she could be outdoors doing what she loved to do, caring for and working with horses. She thought this was a great idea and gave Billy a big hug and thank you.

Though Annie thought it was ridiculous because Mary was so frail, from the day Mary started, it was a success. She had many friends in Milton, Readville, and Hyde Park. Some knew her as the woman they called Mamie and encouraged her in this fight for health. To most she introduced herself as Mary. Eventually, she would be more widely known as Mary Bronsdon or Miss Bronsdon, and she answered to all with a smile.

Among the regular patrons she drove for were some of the wealthier residents of the area, and in some cases, the country: the Wolcott's, the Ackermann's, the Hemenway's, Bishop Lawrence, and the Brooks family.

This was a good deal for both Bronsdon Express and Mary. Billy offered this for her health, but he had grand ideas for making things easier for himself.

He would show Mamie how to do the scheduling of the Milton carriage runs. She already knew many of the clients and was actually friendly with them. They were very well-heeled people, and Billy could not send most of his men, which left the runs up to him or Murch. This could be fine, as long as her health would cooperate.

"Not too much, Mary," he told her. "This is hard work. Let's just see how you hold up."

To understand the names of her favorite horses, you would have to dig into ancient history. The big bay was Bucephalus, and the white one was Pegasus.

Billy and Mamie hitched up Pegasus, and Billy climbed into the back, telling Mamie to drive toward Milton. They spent the afternoon up and down roads and paths, letting Mary get used to being the hackney driver. Billy pointed out houses and names as she silently took in what he said. One good thing was that she knew some of these people, so they were not new places to remember. Later, back at Hamilton Street, Billy explained to Mamie how the board worked and some specifics she should know about the customers.

With her black sailor cap and pea coat with the collar pulled up, Mary drove through Wolcott Square with many trying to figure out who the new guy driving for Bronsdon was.

She had a favorite companion, her dog Prince, who would at times trot along behind her, everyone knew it was Mary. Prince was a very smart pal to Mamie; he knew when it was acceptable to jump up onto the baggage rack and never failed to stop at Paul's Bridge for a cold drink of cold water. She carried a canteen with her and would fill it from the stream when needed. The dog also knew what it meant when Mamie said, "Home, Prince." Without hesitation he would do just as she said, and when she got home, Prince would be lying right by the door, waiting to be fed.

She had found Prince when he was about six months old, abandoned between Wolcott and Cleary Square, looking hungry and filthy with mud. She gave him a sandwich she had with her, and he devoured it. With that

Mamie scooped him up into her carriage and brought him home. He took to her as if this was meant to be. After she washed him, his fur was a beautiful reddish brown, and she suggested aloud, "Why, you look like a prince! And that will be your new name—Prince."

She said many times that it was easier to talk to her horses and pets than to many of her acquaintances.

It wasn't long before word spread through the wealthy and society people, and all were requesting Mary. The more she drove, the better she felt, and within a few years, she was as strong and healthy as anyone could ask for. Rain or shine, dark or light, the woman now known as Miss Bronsdon to some and Mamie to most was always on the job. When asked about her horses, she replied, "I only drive fast steppers." This was not actually work to her, although she did get paid.

After breakfast, she had her first run of the day into Milton. The fresh air, crisp and clean—to Mamie this was heaven, despite how bumpy and rutted most of the roads were. She knew the area very well and was able to avoid some very bad conditions, and her customers knew she was capable. They were delighted to hear Mamie singing as she drove; it made her happy and entertained her riders. There were songs for different seasons and for the holidays; Christmastime and carols were favorites. She always tried getting whoever might be on board to join her.

## Mary Brondson Likes to Dance When She Isn't on Cab Box—Has No Use for Hoppety-Hop Kind— Slide Kind Her Favorite.

### By LAURIE HILLYER.

ONE COLD SNOWY NIGHT a quite happy gentleman descended at the Readville station, noted a cabby bundled in fur cap and coat and observed socially, "Dam cold weather, isn't it, old man?"

The cabby made no response, even to repeated pleasantries, and the traveler consigned him to a warmer land for his aloofness. A woman alighted from the train, hur

Shy she was not, but Mamie, Mary, or Miss Bronsdon still knew her company well enough and respected the boundaries of many. They would be the ones she considered "prudes," but she never named them to anyone.

The new year was 1903, and Mamie was right on her game. A new song that year and one of her favorites to sing when heading to the stable was "Won't You Come Home, Bill Bailey?" In the quiet evening air, Mamie would do verses as if on stage. On a warm afternoon in August of that same year, she would be singing and humming beautifully "In the Good Old Summertime."

Her ability to entertain while whistling a song was memorable as well.

These were the days of the Wright brothers, and the newspapers had some fascinating stories. One thing Mamie always had was a good imagination. She believed in her sense of herself. Driving down a long, straight road with Pegasus, Mamie would talk "Peggy" into going faster and faster—no whip, just talk: "C'mon, Peggy! Go! We'll fly!" And looking through her driving glasses, she would imagine she was flying like Orville Wright.

Other than the fact that she was a woman doing man's work, her life was rather unassuming and enjoyable.

During Mamie's lifetime she went by many names to various groups of friends and patrons, some by nature and some for other reasons. When she started driving for Billy, she was Mary Hickey and hoping to feel better. Soon, her riders were referring to her as Mary Bronsdon, and she was good with that, too. After all, she was driving for the Bronsdon's, and they were her employers.

# CHAPTER 8

# Driving Society

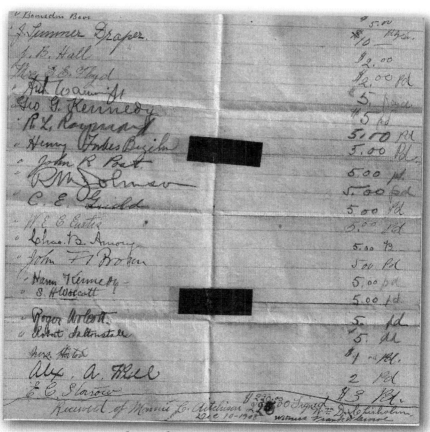

Some of Mamie's money donors

"You must have lots of fun, Miss Brooks," one of her passengers suggested.

Mamie replied, "Last Sunday morning, I was out at five o'clock taking people to early church service through drifts of snow." She had a great sense of humor and could go on talking about the difficulties of being a female driver, but she actually enjoyed a bit of difficulty—"It makes me stronger," she'd say.

Mamie knew all the roads, nooks, and crannies around the Blue Hills and declared that she could read stories in the tracks of bunnies, squirrels, and deer. One very cold and snowy night at Readville Station, a very happy and slightly tipsy gentleman noticed a cabby in a fur hat and coat, all bundled up and saying, "Damn cold, isn't it, old man?"

The man suggested that the cabby "Consign yourself to a warmer place."

Just then, a woman getting off the train headed to the carriage and said, "Aren't you half-frozen, Mamie?"

Mamie answered, "Not at all."

The man looked puzzled. He straightened up, approached Mamie, and said, "Beg pardon, lady."

There were many hazards to driving horses with a carriage besides the fact that horses are incredibly strong and easily spooked. On the morning of September 17, 1907, a fireman at the Readville firehouse and a friend of Mamie's was rushing off to a fire and hadn't attached the horse properly. Just when he jumped to the seat, a loud bang spooked the team. Freddy Hawley missed the seat and was then pulled over the dashboard before he could get his feet on it. The one witness said he was able to make an attempt at running behind the team for about twenty-five yards. He then slid to the ground and was dragged to his death. Billy had to console Mamie, as she was very shaken by this event.

By 1908, Mamie, now known by many, had gained a loyal patronage of passengers. Finding that the postal carrier out of Readville had lost his horse and carriage in an accident and was struggling to make mail deliveries, Mamie organized a fund-raiser, asking for donations from her wealthy patrons, most of whom were on Mr. Chisholm's delivery route as well.

# Woman Cabby Gets Readville's Society Trade

Miss Mary Brondson, the only licensed woman cab driver in New England, has captured society's custom in Readville, where she drives to and from the depot. She has among her regular patrons the Wolcotts, the Rackemanns, the Hemenways, Bishop Lawrence, the Halls and the Brooks family. Miss Brondson chose this out-door employment because of ill-health. She drives only fast steppers.

Mrs. Wolcott—$10.00

Mrs. Chickering—$10.00

Miss Brooks—$10.00

Oak Ames—$10.00 (he noted that he does not use his services)

Clifford Brigham—$5.00

Felix Rackemann—$10.00

Mrs. Augustus Hemenway—$10.00

J. Sumner Draper—$10.00

Alex A. Will—$2.00

Robert Saltonsthal—$3.00

There are twenty-one names of donors on her note pad. Mamie collected $220 and was able to present Mr. Chisholm with a horse and carriage supplied by Bronsdon Brothers. Soon after, she received a thank-you note signed, "Again thanking you and beg to remain sincerely yours, W. D. Chisholm."

Miss Bronsdon driving her steed

Another patron of Mamie's who signed on to donate five dollars to Mr. Chisholm was A. L. Rotch, the man who conceived the idea of the Blue Hill Observatory. Rotch graduated from MIT in 1884, and being from Boston society, he built the first small stone observatory in 1885 with $3,500 of his own money. On January 31, 1885, he celebrated the opening with fireworks that could be seen for miles and caused some concern. This was a man who loved to talk while Mamie was driving, always about the weather. Much of his banter was quite technical as he got his thoughts together for the day, but Mamie still found it interesting. Mr. Rotch was one of the men the Wright brothers consulted about weather conditions.

Mr. Abbott Lawrence Rotch, having been well educated in meteorology as a young man, had the idea of monitoring weather atop Blue Hill. In about 1885 he founded the Blue Hill Meteorological Observatory, within sight of Boston, Massachusetts.

One day while driving through Milton, Mr. Rotch asked Mary if she had ever flown a kite. She immediately said, "Yes. Have you?" Then he began to talk about the use of kites and balloons to record data about the upper atmosphere and further explained about the air flight trials of the Wright brothers. They, along with other aviation pioneers including French-born Octave Chanute, wrote many exchanges of information in support of the Wrights.

Upon returning from an extended trip to Europe, Mr. Rotch was very talkative while Mamie was driving. He was telling her about his trip to France and about seeing the Wright brothers fly their aeroplane. Mr. Rotch was explaining how the machine lifted off the ground and flew like a bird. He was fascinating to listen to.

He only knew her as Miss Bronsdon and was so happy she enjoyed his talk. Mr. Rotch showed Mary a coin he told her came from the Wright brothers' demonstration outside Paris, France. The brothers showed their invention to the French government in 1907 in Le Havre, and Mr. Rotch had given Orville some advice on the lift near water. He explained that getting too close to the cooler air off water might cause the craft to descend without recovery. Rotch told Mary that Orville flipped him a coin from his pocket with a smile and thanked him with a tip of his hat. After paying the fare, he handed Mamie that coin. She left it with me in fine condition.

Wright brothers' coin

It was just a year later that she was collecting for Mr. Chisholm when Mr. Rotch had the original two-tower building torn down and erected a new three-tower observatory that still stands today.

Driving Miss Brooks was as much fun as driving anyone, with her being a children's author and very popular throughout the country in the late 1800s and into the twentieth century. Mamie knew her as Amy, and she would at times use Mamie to tell her stories to as she was working on them. Sometimes Miss Brooks sat up front so Mamie could hear her better. During the period between 1905 and 1912 or so, Amy was involved in writing and illustrating a classic book series called Dorothy Dainty. Mamie would get excited just knowing she would be driving Amy and would try to remember what the last story had been. This was a thirteen-book series, and Mamie was hearing some of what would eventually be published. She felt very special.

Miss  Book Between 1900 and 1907, Amy had also written some books called the Randy books, with a character named Prue. These were also classics. As the series progressed, Mamie wondered if the character Prue could

Brooks/Prue

possibly be her. Well, not herself, but Prue's characteristics made it seem possible. You see, the series was based in Boston, Prue was country raised, and the jest was that Randy didn't want Prue to become "citified." The book series is available still today.

# CHAPTER 9

# Taxed and Licensed

AFTER YEARS OF DRIVING, MAMIE was required to obtain a license in 1914. Billy explained the reason and told her to use Mary C. Aitchison as her name on record.

The government had established a new income tax the year before, through the Revenue Act of 1913. Now, even though Mamie would not make enough money to have to actually pay the tax, she would have to be licensed. Billy profited from all the drivers he employed and had to find ways to, shall we say, "transfer funds economically." Mamie trusted Billy. As the license was issued to the driver with the livery stable's address, accounting done properly could keep Mary off the ledger. The tax was basically 1 percent on incomes of $3,000 for a single individual and $4,000 per married couple. In 1916 the tax doubled to 2 percent with same rules. But by this time, the country needed money for the war.

When Mamie went in to apply for the license from the city, it caused some excitement in Pemberton Square in downtown Boston. The inspector of carriages protested, "No, you don't want a license. Driving a carriage is too hard work for a woman!"

"Thanks," Mamie replied. "I've been earning a living better than ten years with a pair of reins!"

She passed the physical requirements with ease and was assigned badge number 1486. The license was signed by the first Boston police commissioner, Stephen James O'Meara, who had been sworn in as head of the department in 1906. The Boston police had been taken over by the Commonwealth of

**ONLY LICENSED WOMAN CABBY IS IN READVILLE**

*Boston Journal        Oct. 9 /14.*

**Miss Mary Brondson Has Made Good at Her Profession, Which She Likes Because It Keeps Her Out in the Open Air.**

Massachusetts in 1885 to stop the corruption caused by the city's Irish population. Then Mayor Michael Curley, an Irish politician, used his heritage to influence city policies during his term.

Stephen O'Meara was not a politician and worked tirelessly to keep Boston out of corrupt hands. Because he was Irish, it was thought that he would keep the population happy but not be involved with political issues. By 1915 O'Meara had made the department into one of the top three forces in the country. The men knew they were on top of their game and wanted better wages. Through early 1918 the commissioner yielding great respect, was able to fend off the demands to a later time. Then by August, 1918 the demands and talk of unionizing began. By fall there was bargaining taking place and raises were offered that would only affect about one quarter of the department.

Commissioner O'Meara died suddenly in December 1918.

August, 1919 *"The Boston Social Club"*, now the Boston Police Department asked for charter in the AFL, they were accepted immediately. By September 9, the strike began. It was strongly felt that, had O'Meara still been in charge, the strike would not have happened.

On July 13, 1914, Mamie became "the only licensed woman driver in New England if not the United States," as reported by the *Boston Journal* on October 9, 1914.

I have Mamie's original licenses from 1914 to 1915 and 1915 to 1916 and the news clippings she was so proud to have.

Mary Hickey, Mary Bronsdon, Mary Aitchison, and eventually Mary McDonough...well, Mamie. To know her was to understand that that name fit perfectly. Her father began calling her Mamie as it was easier for him to say, a term of endearment. When he would sternly talk to "Mary," it still sounded like Mamie. Later, to avoid confusion, she began telling friends, "Just call me Mamie."

Mary Aitchison showed income, but very little, and Mamie showed none.

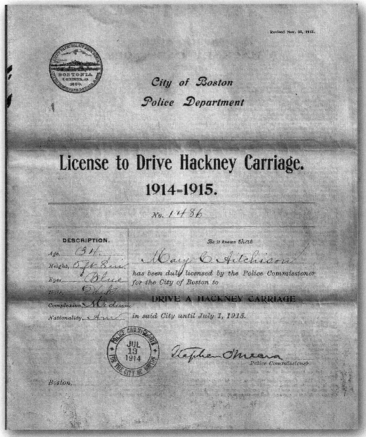

Hackney license 1914–1915

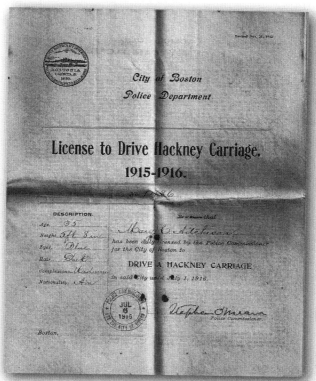

Hackney license 1915–1916

# CHAPTER 10

# Driving History

MAMIE WAS NOW A LICENSED cabby, wearing her leather driving coat and black sailor's cap with her medallion proudly displayed on its brim. She was no longer frail. At 150 pounds and hard as nails, she could swing a trunk and flash her whip, or "snapper" as Mamie briskly referred to it, as well as any man around. Not at all masculine, she had become strong, lean, and much sturdier than most women.

While driving many notable people during her career, Mamie was kept very busy during the Grand Circuit races at Readville Race Track, and it was considered a novel experience to be driven by a woman.

She drove a double buggy, meaning it had two seats, front and rear, with a closed back and folding top, open sides, and four wheels. There was a rack between the rear wheels for luggage and at times freight to be picked up and delivered elsewhere for Bronsdon Brothers Express, as the plaque that was also on her hat proudly displayed.

Her carriage did have side-spring suspension; after all, Mamie was driving high society, and they paid quite handsomely. She carried extra coats and a heavy blanket for anyone needing to be warmer, since the open-air carriages were unheated.

There was no shortage of society members living in Milton near the foot of Blue Hill and in the Hyde Park area. Some of these people had historical ties to the area and beyond, and Mamie found her way to take part.

The area of Milton had a very quiet, rural feel though it was just a short carriage ride to Readville Depot and the train bound for bustling downtown

Boston. Magnificent and elaborate homes were set on picturesque landscapes, with all the day's amenities. Many still stand today.

One such family who kept Mamie quite busy was the Wolcotts—Governor Wolcott and family. Roger Wolcott was born in Boston on July 13, 1847. His father, Joshua Huntington Wolcott, was a successful businessman associated with A. A. Lawrence in textiles. The family is descended from Connecticut's founding father, Oliver Wolcott. As a boy Roger traveled through Europe with his family as he continued his studies. Returning from Europe, he entered Harvard College, graduating in 1870, and then Harvard Law School, graduating in 1874. He was then admitted to the Suffolk bar.

On September 2, 1874, he married Edith Prescott, great-granddaughter of Colonel William Prescott, who commanded the rebel troops at the Battle of Bunker Hill and would be noted in history as conveying to his soldiers the order "Do not fire until you see the whites of their eyes." William Prescott, born in Groton, Massachusetts, February 20, 1725, Died October 13, 1795.

Mr. and Mrs. Roger Wolcott honeymooned in Europe for a year. When they returned in 1875, Wolcott started his own law firm. He dabbled in politics as city councilor and in the state legislature while caring for his elderly father.

In 1885 he was offered the Republican nomination for mayor of Boston, but he declined because of his father's ill health. He cared for his father until his death in 1891.

Roger then became active in Massachusetts politics and became the thirty-sixth lieutenant governor, serving from 1893 to 1897. He assumed the duty of acting governor with the death of Governor Frederic T. Greenhalge in 1896 and was elected the thirty-ninth governor in November, serving from 1897 to 1900. He was very popular but decided not to run for reelection in 1900, opting for a trip to Europe with his family, leaving in May of 1900. Upon returning to campaign for his fellow Republicans, Roger suddenly became ill with typhoid fever in November and died December 21, 1900.

Mary, as Mrs. Wolcott lovingly referred to Mamie, was very fond of her, and she was the Wolcott's requested driver. There was little surprise when she was invited to the wedding of Cornelia Wolcott to Reverend Samuel Smith Drury, vice rector of the elite prep school Saint Paul's Academy in Concord,

New Hampshire. The wedding was held on April 18, 1911, at Saint Stephen's Church. It was a grand affair, with all of society attending from near and far. Mary proudly attended, mingling with the Peabody's, Bigelow's, Loring's, and Endicott's, to name just a few. The multitude of guests were received by Mrs. Roger Wolcott at her residence on Commonwealth Avenue. The newlywed couple left immediately after to honeymoon in Europe until June. They would live at Saint Paul's Academy, where Reverend Drury succeeded Reverend Dr. Ferguson as head rector for the next twenty-seven years until his death in 1938.

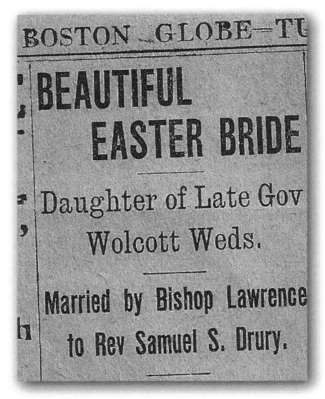

Notable patrons of Mamie's carriage service lived in the vicinity of the Blue Hills. She was requested by families such as the Hemenway's, the Eustise's, and the family of a man named Bishop Lawrence.

William Lawrence, "the Bishop," was Harvard educated, as was his family. He was a very stern and direct man without exception, but he enjoyed his

Immediately after the ceremony there was a reception at the home of the bride's mother on Commonwealth av. The interior was decorated with a profusion of Easter lilies.

The young couple were assisted in receiving by Mrs Roger Wolcott : Mrs Drury. Rev and Mrs Drury will sail immediately for Europe, where they will remain until June. Upon their return they will make their home at St Paul's school, Concord.

Among those invited were:

Mrs Mary (Bronsdon) Atchison
Mr & Mrs Thomas Barbour
Mrs Franklin Barnes
Mr & Mrs Spaulding Bartlett
Mr Henry Forbes Bigelow

Miss Katharine Loring
Miss Louisa Loring
Miss May Loring
Mrs Wm Caleb Loring
Rev & Mrs A W Martin
Miss Fanny P Mason
Miss McGregor
Mr & Mrs R McIver
Dr & Mrs G H Monks

travels with Mamie. If he was quiet, she would whistle; if he was talkative, she would listen. They both enjoyed these times.

Charles Bean Amory of Civil War fame was a member of the Massachusetts Twenty-Fourth Volunteers with some rich war history. He was one of six veterans invited to take part in the fiftieth anniversary of the Battle of Gettysburg in 1913. His home was on Atherton Street near Curry College, and Mamie was his regular cabby to the Readville Station. One day, he was brimming with excitement, riding to the station to head south for a few days, telling Mamie about some events of the war. This became a regular theme for Mr. Amory as he had written a book a few years earlier. *"A Brief Record of the Army Life of Charles B. Amory"*. Talking of his army career, he would tell his story to Mamie as he recalled details. She was engrossed by his story and looked forward to driving him until his death in 1919.

When General Nelson A. Miles was in Readville, Mamie was his driver. Miles was a Massachusetts boy, born on August 8, 1839, and raised on a farm in Westminster. As a young man, he moved to Boston, working as a clerk in a crockery while attending night school, studying all aspects of the military. When the Civil War broke out, Miles joined the Union army on September 9, 1861, as a volunteer. He fought in many battles, becoming a lieutenant in the Twenty-Second Regiment of the Massachusetts Volunteer Infantry. He was commissioned a lieutenant colonel of the Sixty-First New York Volunteer Infantry Regiment on May 31, 1862, and became a full colonel following the Battle of Antietam.

After the war ended in 1865, he was appointed commandant of Fort Munroe, Virginia, where former Confederate president Jefferson Davis was being held. Wounded four times during the Civil War, he was awarded brevet brigadier general on March 2, 1867, in the regular army. He then became commander of the Fifth US Infantry Regiment in March of 1869. Soon after this, he was sent west, commanding in the Indian Wars, and he played a role in all campaigns from 1874 to 1875.

During 1876 and 1877, his regiment scoured the northern plains searching for the Lakota tribe, which had massacred General Custer at Little Big Horn, and forced them onto the reservation. He then rallied his troops to march across Montana during the winter of 1877 to capture Chief Joseph.

The period from 1881 to 1884 had Miles commanding the Department of California. Miles was promoted again in 1885 or 1886 to lead the Department of Missouri. Soon after, he became commander of the Department of Arizona in the fight against Geronimo. In 1890 Miles was in command of the troops that killed Sitting Bull.

His political allies rewarded him with a brevet major general for his action in Virginia in 1863. On July 23, 1892, he was awarded the Medal of Honor for gallantry at Chancellorsville. A bloody battle lasting more than a week with heavy loses to both sides.

From 1894 to 1895, he was commander for the Department of the East, and later in 1895, he was appointed commanding general of the US Army.

After forcing the Spanish to surrender in Cuba, he personally led the invasion of Puerto Rico. In 1900, President Theodore Roosevelt called Miles "a brave peacock."

Just a few years later, in 1903, he was forced into retirement at age sixty-four. Although in 1917, at age seventy-seven, he offered to serve in World War I, President Woodrow Wilson turned him down.

Mamie sent Miles best wishes on his eighty-third birthday, and in August 1922 she received a thank-you note handwritten and signed "Nelson A. Miles."

Billy had been told that Miles was coming, and he sent Mamie purposely, as he knew the general would be surprised at a woman driver. He did tell her who she was picking up, and she was thrilled.

Mamie was there just as the train came in and pulled alongside the platform to wait. Then out came the general, and he was very easy to pick out, being quite boisterous about how his bag was handled. As Mamie approached, he sensed oddly that this was a woman working as a baggage handler. Then she took the bag and introduced herself as "Mary, Mary Bronsdon General Miles, I'll be your driver today."

He smiled and told her to "lead on, my good driver. I'll be heading to the racetrack." She asked if he minded a quick stop back at the barn to fix a halter strap on Pegasus, which was fine by him. Her real reason was that Billy wanted to meet him and had asked her to do this, the general having been the commanding officer of the army at one time and honored for his actions during the Civil War. Billy felt a bit of connection with Camp Meigs having been such an important part of the victory. When they pulled into the livery area, Billy was waiting and looking busy when Mamie asked to introduce them.

General Miles was a big man both in size and stature as he stepped off the carriage to meet Billy, or William, as he was introduced by Mary. They shook hands, and there was a noticeable difference in height: Billy was only about five foot six, and the general was over six feet. But Billy's hands were large, strong, and rough with callouses, and he had a good grip. Miles was impressed.

Billy offered a refreshment while Mary fixed the strap, and Miles gladly accepted. There was a cold pitcher of water that Annie had put out with some fancy glasses. He offered a drink and said, "How about a little taste of Jamaica?" The general's head twisted quickly as he asked about what he meant by "taste of Jamaica."

So Billy told him about the coffee shop owner having a sea captain connection, explaining how his coffee beans came from Jamaica, while sipping some fine rum he acquired from Brewer. Even General Miles was impressed by the quality of this elixir.

Soon Mary came calling that she was ready. "So we'll be off. We're just going right down the road a bit." While they were getting up, Billy suggested they hang on a moment, and he pulled a flask out of the desk, saying he'd fill it for the general to take. Miles held up his right hand in a *stop* motion while reaching into his left breast pocket and pulling out a flask of his own. He suggested that it must have dried up during the train trip, and it would be wonderful of Billy to refill it with some rum.

General Nelson Miles died in 1925.

Mamie certainly had many interesting and famous patrons, and she enjoyed talking of them later in life. Another military moment was sometime in December of 1915, just before Christmas. Mamie had two men going to the racetrack, which was odd this time of year. She knew as well that Billy had picked up a crate at Sturtevant Fan Company's Hyde Park factory at the beginning of the week and brought that to the track as well.

One of the men, Eugene Foss, was the son-in-law of B. F. Sturtevant, the company founder. The other, Grover C. Loening, had been hired as an aeronautical engineer. He had been in the military in San Diego. They designed a V-8 water-cooled engine that was built by Sturtevant. It could achieve 140 horsepower and could be mounted on an aircraft.

While driving these fares, it being Christmas season, Mamie began singing her holiday collection. The men protested loudly, as they were trying to have a meeting. She stopped.

Their project made a loud, horrible noise and failed miserably, and Mamie would smirk every time she told this tale.

Mamie loved to whistle and was quite good. One clear September evening, she was driving under moonlight in a lonely area near Blue Hill. This night, as she approached the main road, another station driver came along behind her. He told of being attacked by his fares who were joined by someone hiding in the woods, and he was robbed. After that, Miss Bronsdon traveled armed.

# CHAPTER 11

# Woman of Wits

ON A VERY COLD AND stormy night on the road from Ponkapoag, Mamie came upon a young girl half-frozen. She put the child in her carriage and brought her home to warm up with hot chicken broth. When the girl had warmed some, she was able to tell Mamie that her name was Annabel. She had gotten lost coming home from school and did not know her last name. Once Annabel was warmed, Mamie brought her to the Hyde Park police station, where her father picked her up, although he never did thank Mamie.

Ponkapoag is in the western area past the Blue Hills. The name means "a spring that bubbles from red soil." This was a Native American plantation that was originally part of Dorchester, then established in 1657 by a clan of the Massachuset tribe, part of the Algonquian family, dating back more than five thousand years. There are accounts of some 90 percent of these coastal tribes dying of European plague in the early 1600s. This camp was originally used for winter housing away from the wind off the ocean, where they lived during the summer.

Despite her strenuous work, Mamie was always a smiling young lady, intense and businesslike, but the most obliging and helpful of people, except with news photographers, who basically had to ambush her. She loved what she did and would continue as long as possible.

Mamie enjoyed her gateway to nature. Heading out of Readville and into Milton just before Paul's Bridge where it was bordered by Fowl Meadow, tall trees with many branches formed a canopy above the street. That was "the gateway," and in the summer, when it was full of leaves, it would be a tunnel.

The area was teeming with waterfowl, ducks, and geese, and there'd be pheasant and turkeys as well. She would take advantage of an opportunity to put a fat bird on her table.

Driving society had other advantages. Most of the wealthy didn't cook for themselves. They would have a cook on their staff. On many occasions she would leave with a full belly or something for her to eat while driving. Cooking was done mostly with wood, and Mamie loved the smell of burning wood mixed with roasting meat coming from the kitchen chimney as she drove up for her fare. Then she would go check to see what it was she had detected cooking. Sometimes she'd take a sandwich wrapped in a napkin with her.

But this cabby liked to cook, and being on the run so much, she had to fend for herself. Her go-to easy meal was a fat pigeon from her coop by the back door. Cleaned and in a pan, it took just a few minutes. Along with soda bread, strawberry jam, and thick sweet cream, it was a favorite.

Gardening was a natural love of Mamie's, but she didn't have time for a big garden while driving, so she kept a small area adjacent to the pigeon coop. Carrots, lettuce, and cucumbers were good enough. There were chickens as well, but they were kept for eggs, as long as they were producing. When they stopped laying, then they were Sunday chicken dinner.

Four o'clock in the morning would find her making coffee. She loved it with cream and sugar. Breakfast was two soft-boiled eggs and buttered wheat toast. On very cold mornings, there might be oatmeal, too, if her schedule and weather permitted.

Rain or snow didn't matter; she had to do her work. There were times when her fares would cancel on arrival, but she always made her appointments. Working seven days a week was normal, but she found time for enjoying herself. Being athletic, Mamie enjoyed sports like baseball.

Her animals were her life, as they understood her kindness fully.

She had no time for politics.

One news story of the time read, "Mary Bronsdon likes to dance when she isn't on the job and has no use for hoppty-hop stuff, glide kind her favorite."

In 1786, long before Mamie began traveling the roads, a trip from Boston to New York took about six days. Then by 1826, with new toll roads running between large cities, travel time improved, and New York could be reached from Boston in just a day and a half.

The southern section of Massachusetts had some of the better roads in the country at the time. Most of them began as animal trails that became wider as the natives walked them. As the population grew and horse travel became the transportation of the day, the paths became roads. Mamie traveled on the more established roads, but there were many small paths, and knowing the area as she did, she would use these shortcuts when needed.

CHAPTER 12

# Billy, Murch, and Jack

BRONSDON BROTHERS EXPRESS WAS WELL established with a good name.

Billy and Murch were working hard and having a great time. They had three depot carriages, two freight haulers, and two delivery wagons for loads of lumber, coal, and stone for building materials.

The Bronsdon boys were prepared.

They had a herd of eighteen horses of all sizes and breeds. Billy was as good with horses as anyone. Murch drove a freight wagon, but his job was mainly the financial aspect, making sure the cash came in and bills were paid.

Just a short walk southeast of the Bronsdons, toward Milton and Fowl Meadow, lived John McDonough, known to most as Jack. He did a little of everything and was very good at just about any endeavor he challenged himself with. Having acquired quite a bit of real estate in and around Readville, Jack owned most of the area adjacent to the meadow north to Chester Street. This was where he built his own house and small outbuildings, acquiring wagon-loads of lumber along the railroad. Loads of would shift on railcars and at times break loose, scattering all types of wood. The train men were not responsible for picking the lumber up. They would alert Jack to the location, and he would reward them with a bottle of whiskey. Many times, he'd share the bottle.

Some of the lumber would be heading to the lumber yard along the avenue just before Wolcott Square, but the owner, E. F. Cutter, a tall Yankee from New Hampshire, gave no reward, so the yardmen said nothing.

With growing children and so much business, the house was too small for Annie. After she discussed it with Billy, they decided to build another house at the end of his lot. Billy contacted Jack McDonough to see if he could help with this project. After seeing the area Billy wanted to use, Jack told him that the lot was not of sufficient size for what he proposed. Jack had an idea and suggested to Billy a three-decker house, which would give Billy the living space he wanted. At first Billy thought maybe Jack had been drinking a little early. But no, he was serious, and he told Billy that if he could sell him some of the lumber and if Billy would hire four good men, he would help with this project by directing the construction. They agreed on a fee of $300 for Jack. Jack would also salvage and charge Billy for whatever lumber he could supply for the job. It was a good deal for both parties, and they got the project underway.

It took Jack and the crew about a year to complete the house, which was quite tall and looked out of place. There were not many houses in Readville that were built this way. You had to go into the crowded city to see three-deckers that were built for the same reason: a small footprint with plenty of living space.

This house design was easy to heat, especially if you lived on the second floor.

Annie wasn't sure.

It did look odd, but Mamie was there with Annie this warm sunny afternoon in August, and Mamie asked if she could go to the top of the world and see what it was like. She bounded up the winding stairway to the third floor and went right out onto the front porch, looking across toward Readville Race Track, the original site of Camp Meigs. Just 150 feet away, she could see the massive granite stones with huge cannons mounted on them used for training troops. It was an impressive site.

She yelled to Annie, "You must see this! It's glorious, my dear!"

Annie made her way up the stairs not at all as her sister had, and breathless from the hike up, declared that she couldn't manage those stairs. Mamie took her hand and walked her to the porch. Though at first she was frightened by the height, she turned to Billy and said, "Spectacular! I can see things that I didn't even know were there." With that Billy moved his family in, and Annie was very happy.

Jack had a charge of goose bumps run right down his back when Mary pronounced the view "glorious." He had known her for several years, but he not paid attention to her, as he was always busy doing things that men usually do. But on this day, he saw and heard a different person. Maybe he had never really listened before.

Jack told Mary that he had an abundance of vegetables; in fact, his vines of cucumbers and tomatoes were the best he'd had in three years, and he suggested that she come and take some whenever she liked.

With a thank you and a nod, she said, "I'll be by later today."

She was off with her carriage, headed to Milton. Her fare was at the Eustis estate; she was taking Miss Eustis to the train depot. Then she would pick up patrons going to the racetrack.

The land the track was on had been purchased in 1895 by the New England Trotting Horse Breeders Association, and the track officially opened August 25, 1896, under the name Readville Trotting Park. There was a grandstand, a clubhouse, a restaurant, and a hotel. The *New York Times* applauded the track for having some of the best exhibitions of any track in the country. Later being a motorized race track before closing in May 1937.

On race days, Mary was very busy before and after the events, as were many hackney carriage drivers. Mary knew her regular customers very well, and she would always pick them up ahead of strangers by calling out as if she was there just for them. She could also tell by the tip amount who had won money at the track that day. These were very profitable days for all of Readville, with money being spent in the area. Mamie wouldn't take any tips that were more than they should have been from patrons who won money at the track—at least not from the local ones.

And then there were always the drunks whom she wouldn't pick up unless they were well known to her.

# Travel through Time

JACK LIKED TO FISH THE Neponset River, and he had easy access from his home. There was almost always some water in the swampy meadow. If there had been enough rain or snow runoff, it would fill like a lake. It was basically a huge bog. Alongside, the river meandered from its headwater in Walpole near Bird Pond. In 1659 a sawmill was erected at this location; in 1710, the F.W. Bird family purchased the mill.

The Neponset River flows east to south from Walpole through Norwood, Canton, Westwood, Dedham, Boston, Milton, and Quincy, where it empties into Quincy Bay and then on into Boston Harbor.

Having grown up here and spent many hours traveling up and down the river in his canoe, Jack had locations for many species of fish and reptiles.

Native people had traveled the river for some five thousand years. Written history began in the early 1600s, with the natives traveling to Boston Harbor for fur trading. In 1626, some years before Boston came to be, David Thompson established a trading post on a harbor island now known as Thompson Island.

Earth has been in a constant state of change since its creation. Many years ago, during the Ice Age, the entire landscape of New England as we know it today did not exist. As the planet warmed, the glacier retreated, and the water flowed away to form an ocean. It left huge mineral and soil deposits called drumlins, an Irish word meaning "little ridges." These would become the many islands in Boston Harbor that we know today. There were great numbers of natives at the time, an estimated thirty to fifty thousand in Massachusetts alone, and the area was teeming with valuable fur-bearing wildlife.

There were many clans, but Thompson referred to them as Neponset people. They came and went by the river, traveling farther inland for winter and setting up summer camps along the shoreline for many years. Their main homesite was at Neponset Falls, which is where the river becomes tidal. It was called Unquity Quisset, meaning "headwater meets tidewater," and it would bring fish in from the bay with the changing tides.

This was the site of the first grist mill, built in 1634 by Colonel Israel Stoughton to grind corn. Food was in short supply, and after setting up the mill, he was able to purchase some corn from the natives to grind. This would save some from starvation.

The natives knew it was time to plant their corn when the alewife came home to spawn, now mature at five years and swimming up rivers and streams by the millions back to the lakes and ponds where they'd hatched. After laying anywhere from fifty to one hundred thousand eggs per fish, they'd make their way back to open ocean until the next year. Early people depended on the fish for food, and scraps were used as fertilizer.

Later in spring came the much bigger and plentiful striped fish that could make the bay shine like silver. We call them striped bass today. Some were as long as five feet and weighed one hundred pounds or more. They had sweet, white meat thicker than a man's arm. The people learned the soil was warm enough to plant their beans when these fish arrived.

Downriver from the falls, the bay was full of clams, mussels, oysters, and even lobster.

They traveled upriver toward the Blue Hill area for hunting and trapping. The fur was of good quality, and Thompson made much money as word spread. Boston wasn't far off, as the speculation of land and plentiful bounty was drawing men to settle and build futures. The Neponsets soon sold this prosperous land to the white settlers for what they could and moved.

Traveling along Churchill's Lane south through Milton and past Blue Hill, you come to Ponkapoag, which means "a spring that bubbles from red soil." This was a relatively shallow pond but there were nice pickerel, bass and thick with sweet sunfish.

Jack loved to travel the river early in the morning while it was very calm, just as the sun came up. The air was crisp with the smell of rotting leaves, still damp from the night's dew. He'd glide upriver with a baited line trailing behind, fishing for breakfast. One of his favorite things to fish for was eels—fat eels about two feet long—and he would clean them, strip the skin off, and smoke them whole.

He could venture as far as Canton against the current, which the canoe cut right through like a knife, but farther up the water moved faster, and there were dams beginning near the mills. There were more dams all the way into Norwood and Walpole, with mills making paper and gunpowder and grinding grains.

Jack knew that eels liked to stay near the base of the dams, catching prey that washed past in the rushing water. When the eels were plentiful, he could scoop them with a dip net and then load them in his canoe. They wiggled all over and made a slimy mess, but the payoff of smoked flesh was worth it. He would have a dozen or so in about an hour and only took what he could use, trade, or give to friends.

Jack knew a great spot for smelts in late winter and early spring—down at the lower mills by the Walter Baker chocolate factory. Below the dam the smelt would come to spawn, and they made a great feed. They were small and sweet, and he ate them bones and all, rolled in flour and fried in lard.

It was easier to drive his wagon down here in the winter. Some years, the river would freeze, and Jack would walk it to set traps, but most knew not to trust the ice entirely with the water moving underneath. To fall through would surely mean drowning in the current.

# CHAPTER 14

# Jack McDonough

OVER THE NEXT FEW DAYS, Mamie made it down to Jack's place. Coming back from Milton, just past Fowl Meadow, was Forest Street. It was the first street on the left entering Readville, really not much more than a dirt path just wide enough for a carriage. This went from Milton Street all the way down to the racetrack, traveling behind attorney Harry Dean's house. Jack was just a bit farther along.

Jack McDonough's house 1920

Mamie looked around for him but assumed he was out and about, as there was no sign of him, and he lived alone. Driving back to Hamilton Street by way of Stanley Street, there came Jack with a big load of horse manure from the Bronsdon stable. This was a help to Billy, and Jack loved the fertilizer.

Now in August, when planting was finished he always spread manure on his plots for next season. It made turning easier in spring, and the beds were full of earthworms. He kept a long row with a trench in various parts of the garden, always two feet wide and two feet deep. These trenches would gradually fill each year with garden debris and garbage along with lots of horse manure. Jack would later say that it was his secret to growing with deep, rich soil; the entire garden had been trenched this way over the years.

John M. McDonough—Jack—was quite the character. Tall, slim, strong, and very smart, he could explain how to plant gardens, care for animals, or build a house. One thing that Jack was noted for and very proud of was his green thumb. The area around his property was prolific with garden beds. His strawberries were memorable, and it was said that Jack could grow plants from a rock. He was ornery and self-centered did things his way, lived alone, and liked to drink.

Jack had it all.

He was born in Readville on May 7, 1877, in a house on River Street across from Mother Brook. Jack's mother and father, John and Ellen McDonough, were both born in Ireland.

He had two brothers: Sylvester, born before Jack was a year older; and Patrick Henry, five years younger than Jack.

Some of the McDonoughs' property had originally belonged to his father, who'd acquired the land in trade for his labor. Land was plentiful, but actual money was scarce, so bartering was an economical solution.

Mamie was always so busy she really didn't have time for much else. There was a routine to her life, and she was diligent about keeping her schedule, working for Bronsdon Brothers, and knowing her patrons very well.

Jack had in him "the way of the land." He just seemed to know what to do with most anything in nature. His plants were beautiful. Tomatoes were red, ripe, and delicious. Cukes were bright green and crunchy, just what Mamie

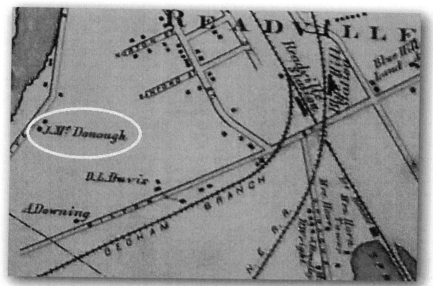

Jack's place of birth

needed to make a batch of pickles. She told Jack that after she'd made a big crock full, she would bring him some. With that, Jack walked way over by his summer screen house and pulled a big handful of fresh dill weed.

Mamie loved the smell of fresh dill, and she could smell it clear across the garden. She told Jack that was just what was needed, and he shyly told her, "I have a weakness for dill pickles, my dear."

With a basket of cucumbers and a dozen tomatoes, she was off to see if Annie wanted to help with pickle making. As she was leaving, Jack suggested that she try a tomato sandwich with salt, pepper, and just a bit of dill leaf.

To some, raising a garden was work. Most everyone grew some sort of vegetables in the summer, with varying degrees of success. Then you take Jack, who could grow almost anything and have it flourish under his watchful eye.

He didn't just grow a few tomatoes. There would be many plants. That was just how he was. Rows would be forty feet in length and three feet wide. He even had a row of sunflowers for their seeds. Jack noticed how much better his chickens laid eggs in winter when sunflower seeds were added to their feed. All his vegetables were planted in the same size beds, and Jack would rotate plants from year to year. When Jack grew his legendary sweet corn, there would be squash vines scattered in between the stalks. Where corn grew one year, bush beans would be planted the next.

Another crop he was fond of was melons. He bought a new variety from a farmer who had come to Boston from France. This farmer's melons were grown on his farm in Hingham from seed called Charantais he'd brought from home. He told Jack that the weather at his field on the ocean was very similar to that at his home in France. There was a market at Faneuil Hall, or the hay market, and that was where Jack got three sweet, juicy melons. After eating one, he saved the seeds to plant and came up with the most spectacular crop of sugar-sweet melons. They were delicious and rewarded Jack with some welcome cash without his having to go downtown. Once people tried them, others showed up from the word of mouth. Jack wasn't very happy with all these people coming around, but the cash was welcome. Besides, these Charantais melons had to be used quickly; they could not be stored.

Town wasn't Jack's forte. He could do it quietly if most of the people would leave him be. He was there to get what he came for, nothing more.

It wasn't that Jack planned to stop for whiskey it just came naturally. He figured that he needed to check the quality of what was available. There were distilleries everywhere, and some had very good liquor.

Jack did frequent one shop, though: the Ames Shovel Company over by Faneuil Hall. He always enjoyed finding a new garden tool, but he bought his old reliable spades and forks here as well. They were manufactured in Easton, about twenty-five miles south of Boston.

Ames shovels were originally made in West Bridgewater by Oliver Ames. He moved the business to North Easton in 1803 before his sons, Oakes and Oliver Jr., took over, and the name became Oliver Ames and Sons. The future held great promise for these men. Whether it was shovels needed for war or for digging fortunes of gold, the name Ames was right there.

Southeastern Massachusetts was full of iron ore, which was used in the local foundries. The entire process was hot, dirty, and dangerous. But it was very profitable, and it made the Ames family quite wealthy.

Oakes was one of Mamie's regular patrons. He rode to the Canton junction to meet his wife every Wednesday. He was a well-dressed, good-looking man and always had a pleasant way about him. He was also a very good tipper.

# CHAPTER 15

# Henry McDonough

Patrick Henry McDonough, born on April 28, 1882, was Jack's younger brother by five years, and Jack was a year or two younger than their older brother, Sylvester.

Being the typical eldest son, Sylvester felt he needed to make his own place in the world and found work in South Boston. He fit in nicely on the dock as a longshoreman, and his Irish heritage in South Boston was very helpful.

Jack stayed around home and helped his parents with work and caring for Patrick. There was an obvious problem with his mental capacity, and he needed special treatment.

It quickly became evident that Patrick was much too common a name within Boston's Irish community. There were Patricks, Paddies, and Pats, so he went by Henry to cut down on the confusion in public. His hearing seemed superior, and he missed very little.

John Michael McDonough Sr. had come to find a new life in America. He did all the things that a poor immigrant with a dream should, working tirelessly because that was what he had to offer for a wage. When landowners offered property instead of a wage, John did that work and acquired good lots. Having been a carpenter and farmer back home in Ireland, he could do most anything and became a well-respected builder.

Jack became his man at home and on any job he might pick up around Readville. He didn't feel the need to go off at four in the morning and travel six hours a day to work ten for pay. Work was strictly six days a week. Sunday was for church and catching up on home chores. Jack learned about growing and tending vegetables, fruits, and so much more. He did well for his age.

Their mother, Ellen, worked most all the time John was gone and always had a good meal ready for supper. She taught Sylvester and Jack to read and to write in cursive, and she taught Henry as well.

Henry loved doing many chores that were boring, repetitive, or even difficult, but they brought peace to his mind. Jack soon found that digging the garden, planting seed and chopping firewood were perfect jobs for Henry. There were times Jack had to tell him he could stop.

It was the same with writing. Once Henry had something to read, he wanted to write it—not *about* what he read, but exactly what he read, word for word, in very legible cursive, English.

After John's and Ellen's deaths, Jack made sure that Henry had a place to live and paid for things in advance to ensure he was safe.

About 1948, Henry was living in a home in Quincy. He kept a journal, a hardcover book embossed with *1948* on the cover. Inside it are his meticulously handwritten thoughts and poetry and his keepsakes. It was written cover to cover in very nice cursive and hand printing. Henry wrote every page by his own hand, and there is some amazing prose and some quotes, of which I will share a few.

1948

Possibly by Patrick Henry McDonough, but definitely written by Henry:

*"Strive not to be the sort of a woman who always enters the room, voice first."*

That was at the very front of his journal, and I wonder if it may have been directed at a staff member.

Henry suggested that this was an old Arab proverb, and as I read his thoughts and choice of prose, it makes me wonder more about his intelligence and mind; he had a hidden brilliance.

Proverb:

*He who knows not, and knows not he knows not, is a fool, shun him.*
*He who knows not, and knows he knows not, is a simple, teach him.*

*He who knows, and knows not he knows, is asleep, awaken him.*
*He who knows, and knows he knows, follow him.*

Short saying:

*Long John our seven foot man about town. Has been voted the man you'd*
*most hate to stand behind at a parade. But who you would love to have*
*in front of you bucking a blizzard.*

Political proverb:

*A politician thinks of the next election, a statesman of the next generation.*

The poems and verses are many, and it was hard to decide, so I let Henry
choose.

Henry's choice:

*Out of Never Came True*
*Sometime in every man's dreaming*
*Out of his dreams will arise*
*Faces he thought he'd forgotten*
*Beautiful radiant eyes*
*Days when the roses are swooning*
*Under the glory of June*
*Nights when the hearts went roaming*
*Under the glimmering moon*

Jack and Mamie did more than many of the day for Henry, and after Jack died,
I have a record of Mamie making sure there was a cash deposit made by Jack's
nephew Leon Raiche whom at the time was a custodian at the Coddington
School in Quincy, Massachusetts. Leon sent a note to *Aunt Mamie* acknowl-
edging the deposit to an account for Henry.

# CHAPTER 16

# Bounty of the Land

MAMIE WOULD GO ACROSS PAUL'S Bridge and walk the area adjacent to the river with her dog, Prince, who would be chasing small animals and frogs and often splashing in the river. This area had lots of princess pine, a small, fuzzy plant only about a foot tall. They made nice wreaths for decorations. The ground along the river being very fertile, there were lady slippers, mushrooms, and berries, but what Mamie was looking for most was ginseng root for making tea.

Edith Getchell had first shown this root to Mamie and how to use it to make a tea for medicinal use. It could be used for all kinds of health benefits. The leaves were similar to poison ivy, but the red berries on top would identify the ginseng, and when the berries were red, the root was ready. Poison ivy had small white berries for better identification. The more berries on ginseng, the older the root, and with age came bigger roots. Once out of the ground, where the stem meets the root, there are growth rings. By counting the rings, you could tell how old the plant was. Mamie kept this dried root in her pantry year round.

Spring would find her walking the wooded areas all over, cutting fiddleheads, but their season was short, maybe a week depending on the temperature. These were the curled young shoots of a fern. They had to be taken at just the right time after emerging at about two inches tall before they blossomed out into beautiful shrublike plants. The plants grew about two feet tall and populated shady locations, doing very well in damp, wooded areas near water.

They emerged soon after the skunk cabbage. Gathering these little facts, Jack used them to predict that winter was really over when he saw these strange, shell-like creatures, the skunk cabbage eventually produced flowers that were the source of food for many insects like bees. Jack said he had seen them coming up in late February while he was out hunting rabbit, and on his garden calendar, he recorded that spring did come extra early that year. Being very intelligent, he enjoyed keeping track of various events centered on his growing from year to year: what day the peas emerged, when he got the first tomato flower, and of course, the date he picked his first tomato.

Fiddleheads were only plentiful for a very short time in the spring. They tasted like asparagus, and Jack especially loved them with a little butter and salt. They had a wild flavor that asparagus didn't have, and the fiddles did not make his urine smell rank. The emerging ferns grew wild along riverbanks and in damp, wooded areas. He could pick a bushel basket full in no time, but he had to watch carefully, as once they appeared, they would fern out in a day or two and no longer be edible until next year.

Mushrooms were another of Jack's fortes. He had secret patches that were loaded with hen of the woods mushrooms, which grew in clusters. They were easy to identify, and if you cut out a section, they always came back. Sautéed in butter, they were a great treat. Mamie loved them, too, but her favorite were morels, which Jack could find but not as easily as hens.

There were so many of these mushrooms that Jack could fill baskets, so he went to the library and found a book on drying food. He already made beef jerky, but drying mushrooms to store seemed like a stretch. After reading for some guidance, Jack made an attempt using the oven but with very little heat, just to dry out the moisture. No easy task, as a mushroom is at least 90 percent water.

The first try actually cooked the batch, and they were very tasty. The next tray Jack put in the same way, but this time he left the oven door open. This worked just fine, and now he had a way to put up mushrooms for soup in winter.

There was another vegetable that grew as a tuber, but the plant was a tall flower stalk that developed yellow flowers. To some they looked like sunflowers, but they were actually perennials that produced a yellowish-to-brown-colored tuber that was quite edible. It tasted like a potato with a sweet, nutty flavor.

The original root stock Jack found down near the river, he dug some up for the tall, yellow flowers to add to his garden. When it began to spread, Jack did some research and found it was called a sun root and was very much edible. The plant also went by the name Jerusalem artichoke. It was good in a number of ways, but Jack's favorite was in a chicken stew. Though not a regular cook, he got used to certain foods and prepared them pretty simply.

Spring would bring other bounty to Eastern Massachusetts, as Quincy Bay would be teeming with fish. There was an area near the mud flats with flounder so thick at high tide that they were easily caught before the tide turned and left huge, muddy flats just loaded with soft-shell clams. This was why the flounder came there. At high tide the clams would stretch their necks or siphons to eat plankton while taking in seawater, and while the clams' necks were out, the bottom-feeding fish would eat the clams like they were picking flowers.

Jack had a friend who lived just off Broad Meadow in Quincy, and he had a skiff that Jack could use anytime, for the cost of a few fish. He'd take a tobacco can of night crawlers for bait. They looked enough like clams' necks that Jack would put a weight on his line to fish on the bottom, and he would fill a basket with fish in no time. He had to plan these trips with the tides, and his trusty *Old Farmer's Almanac* had this information. Jack had to be at the shore while the tide was still going out and just before the ebb or slack tide, when the water ran out of rivers and bays, exposing the muddy or sandy bottom. There would be just a stream with barely enough water to float the small rowboat. By the time he got to where he could see the bay, there would be about three feet of water.

Jack had three points to position himself over an area where he had always done well. Then he'd drop an iron bar on a rope to anchor in place. The water would come up to about fifteen feet deep where he sat, going by a rock about fifty feet away. There was no drinking on these trips; he needed to keep balanced and prepared. Once the basket was full, he would pull anchor and row back as quickly as possible. When Jack saw that the tide had finished its flow phase, he had to stop and head in, even if he hadn't filled the basket. Flow is when the tide comes in, flowing and flooding the many bays and rivers once again. This cycle happens twice a day. When the tide is ready to change, it will be at the ebb stage, as the water begins to retreat from shore.

Later, heading home through Milton, he'd stop at the ice house by Turner Pond, clean his catch by the water, and trade a few fillets to ice down the rest. Jack saved the fish carcasses to dry at home and mix with bone meal as fertilizer. Then there were stops all the way home to share some of his bounty. Most stops earned him a shot or two of whiskey.

# CHAPTER 17

# Green Is His Thumb

⤳

JACK MCDONOUGH WAS FRIENDLY WITH all the men at the train depot. He was a drinking buddy, actually, and he was able to acquire many helpful items around their shop. Like the pot-belly stove he used for heating his small hothouse for plants. He was in the right place one day when they were putting a new heat stove in a caboose. One of the men joked, "Hell, throw the old one on your wagon, so I don't have to move it again."

Without hesitation or word, Jack quickly loaded it onto his lumber wagon, took a swig from a whiskey bottle, and handed the bottle over to his joking friend, who was now a bit surprised. Jack climbed on the wagon while loudly saying, "Thanks, Barney. I'll see ya when I see ya," and off he went.

Every January Jack would start planning for the new year's garden, with his latest copy of *The Old Farmer's Almanac* and his *Household and Farmers' Cyclopedia*, sitting in his old glider chair by the warm stove and thinking back to last year's garden and what he might change.

*The Old Farmer's Almanac*, first published in 1792 by Benjamin Franklin, was where Jack learned to follow the moon's phases. He now marked his calendar with what he should plant on a particular day by the moon. He had done this since he could remember and was sure it was working for him; the proof was in his gardens.

People half-joked about Jack being able to grow lettuce out of a rock. One year, he planted some pole beans as he normally did with teepee-style poles as a trellis; once the seeds came up, he added stones all around the plants, and it looked like the beans were growing from stone. But as his luck would have it,

# Green Is His Thumb

Jack in Boston selecting his seeds, March 1, 1957

he also learned that the soil under the rocks stayed wet longer and produced fewer weeds. Jack was impressed with himself. Everyone knew that he grew the best strawberries in the area, possibly in the country. Reading his farmer' cyclopedia and with some years of experience, Jack found that if he spread an area heavily with manure in early spring and left it alone until July, the manure would draw earthworms to feed and loosen the soil, making it easier to turn with his fork. He'd leave the bed to settle until September and rake it smooth.

Jack's strawberry beds were four feet wide and forty feet long. Understanding how to start plants from seed and buy strawberry seed by mail order was key to his success. They needed to be planted in September, as he read the seed had to be scarified, meaning it they to lie in the cold, frozen soil all winter to germinate properly in spring. Once the seed was planted, he put a heavy layer of straw and pine needles on it. Then, in late April the following year, he would move the straw away to reveal tiny strawberry plants in black, rich soil. Come June, the berries would be as big as horse chestnuts.

This was called "Jack's garden." Some would say he was a farmer, and he liked being referred to that way. But Jack was a carpenter, a mason, and a real, all-around jack-of-all-trades. To turn an area for planting, he would use a flat shovel with a long, well-sharpened blade that would easily cut through the soil and roots. Cutting his outline, he'd then work along the inside with quick motions of the shovel, pushing down with his foot and then leaning it forward to break up the soil and pushing down to let the soil come up to separate and settle. He worked in four-foot-by-four-foot sections. The soil was teeming with worms and rich with organic matter, black and fertile.

The meadows were full of wildflowers, and bees were abundant. The environment in Jack's part of Readville was ideal for growing vegetables and fruit. Pears, peaches, apples, and a big mulberry tree were all part of the realm as well.

Mamie and Annie made a nice crock of dill pickles with the cucumbers from Jack. They kept a big clay crock in the root cellar continuously working. There might be pickled cukes or at times sauerkraut made by salting and curing fresh cabbage that could be jarred and used through the winter. Fresh vegetables were nearly impossible to get in the winter, so they would put up jars to be kept in the root cellar.

Once the dill pickles were deemed ready, they were jarred and processed in boiling water, after which they had a shelf life. They'd be used up by the next spring, when the new growing season would begin with fresh vegetables. It was a good life to be living.

Mamie took two nice quart jars of the fresh pickles and walked down to Jack's place, 44 Chester Street, later to become Colchester Street. It was late on a Thursday afternoon in September. When she arrived, again no Jack.

She was just about to put the jars by his door and leave when Jack's little brown cocker spaniel came running out from the garden. He barked once, turned around, and headed back into the garden.

Mamie followed. She thought it was so thick and lush with plants that you could lose a horse in there. Just as that thought crossed her mind, Jack popped up and scared the daylights out of her. They both had a great laugh.

He had just finished planting the strawberries. Mamie suggested that her favorite thing ever was a good, fresh strawberry. She and Annie always put up many jars of strawberry preserves each summer. Jack told her that he had four strawberry beds that he worked. "You know, the plants need to be replaced every three years. The old ones don't do as well after that."

Mamie said, "You learn something new every day."

Nelson, Jack's dog, was looking for attention, so Mamie picked him up, rubbing his neck as they walked back toward the house. Mamie said, "I almost forgot my reason for coming down. I brought you some pickles with lots of dill."

It was about four o'clock, and Jack said, "I'll have some for supper with a can of sardines."

She asked, "Is that all you are having?"

"Yup...well, that and a little whiskey," he replied with a smile.

Mamie said, "Oh, Jack, I have some nice fresh codfish I got from Billy. Please let me make you dinner."

He looked up, squinted one eye, and said, "Fresh cod?"

Mamie smiled and said, "Come on, let's go."

Jack said to wait a minute, and he ran into the house, cleaned up a little, and grabbed an old onion sack. He told her, "One more minute," and disappeared into the garden again, coming out with a bag of potatoes and a couple of onions, telling Mamie he had just pulled them the day before, and they needed to dry in the sun before he brought them to the root cellar. With that, Jack said, "Let's take my wagon." He went to get his horse while Mamie prepped the harness without even thinking about her movements.

Jack watched her as he walked back and said he had never seen a woman do that so easily.

Mamie took the horse by his bridle and finished hitching him up to the wagon. Then she bolted up onto the wagon as Jack climbed on, and Mamie said, "May I take the reins, sir?"

A bit surprised, he just said, "Sure."

"Well, what's this beautiful fellow's name?" Mamie asked.

"Clyde," Jack responded.

Mamie gave a short whistle and a snap of her fingers in the air, and off went Clyde. Jack was impressed.

# CHAPTER 18

# Jack's Readville

JACK OWNED LOTS OF LAND in various parts of Readville, and when he could, he'd build a house to sell. He was smart and shrewd without trying. That was Jack. He was somehow likable, too, but he did like his booze.

He built small outbuildings throughout his garden area, one with a stove for heat and a cot to lie on. He would sit out in the huts planting seed flats and drinking whiskey. This was his hothouse in early spring when it was still too cold to leave the seeded flats or seedlings out to grow. Jack stayed out in the huts to keep the stoves burning and keep the flats warm. He loved his plants. When the fire got low and he was asleep on the makeshift bed getting a chill, he was there to put wood on the fire while nipping at his whiskey.

Jack didn't always use wood. He could pick up coal along the railroad tracks that regularly bounced off rail cars or an errant engine stoker.

His main interest was lumber. He loved to build things. With his mind full while he was building, he was happy but aggressive and difficult to work for. Things had to be done the way he had figured them.

Anyone Jack did work for was always happy, and he was fair. He did more than they expected he was going do, but he never charged more than he quoted.

Jack's property was only about three hundred feet from the edge of Fowl Meadow. The meadow itself was another two hundred yards from the tree line, which was at the banks of the Neponset River, the border of Readville and Milton. Following the river to the left took you under Paul's Bridge and farther on to Boston Harbor, coming out in Dorchester near Quincy Bay.

Jack McDonough with Pegasus

The water runoff from Blue Hill into many small streams running into the river was clear and clean. The Neponset intersected Paul's Bridge, shallow and rocky with a mild current—a good drink for man or beast. The water in this stream ran down from a pond about a mile up in Milton. It was situated next to and running under Blue Hill Avenue and was named Hemenway Pond.

There are many locations around Milton and Readville as well as in downtown Boston that memorialize the Hemenway name.

Augustus Hemenway (1853–1931) was a wealthy philanthropist in the New England area. He donated the Hemenway Gymnasium to Harvard in 1878, expanding it in 1895. He married Harriet Lawrence (1858–1960). She would become the cofounder of the Massachusetts Audubon Society.

At the back of the pond is where the land begins its ascent to Blue Hill. Along Canton Avenue, it intersects close to the Eustis estate with its beautiful gatehouse. Then up the long driveway in front over rolling foothills that lead to the main house.

There is a nice stream that runs down these hills from Big Blue, as it's called, flowing on down to Hemenway Pond with its nice pickerel and perch.

Jack could sit on his piazza and gaze up at the hue of Great Blue Hill. The meadow, flush with all types of game birds, deer, rabbits, and more, was a hunter's paradise. The river had fish and snapping turtles; Jack loved turtle soup. When he hunted, he only took what he needed at the time. This wasn't for sport; this was for food.

There were others hunting these woods and meadows. There were still Native Americans living in the area. They had been pushed farther up onto the hill by the encroaching population, but it was peaceful here for Jack. He was home.

Years when the meadow had high water in the spring, Jack learned that he had better growing results and figured out that the water table was up even under his garden areas. Mamie was quite amazed as Jack told her about his theory, and then she saw the results herself. He truly did have a great gift for and love of growing things.

Jack traveled into the city to order his seed from a store in the market area next to the Ames shovel shop. He would order certain seeds that the store did not stock, but he became like a kid in a candy store come spring when the new seed rack went up.

The area near Faneuil Hall had almost everything Jack needed, though he did not buy much. He was quite frugal and preferred to make, find, or trade most things.

Small distilleries were common in those days, and men had preferences for various types of liquor. Jack was a whiskey man, and there was a shop in Roxbury that he frequented. It was a nine-mile trip home, and Jack would be pretty well liquored up by the time he and Clyde got there, so he got all his choosing and buying or bartering done first.

During the winter or when he was not hauling anything in or out, he would take the train. He still drank his whiskey on the train, but it was faster, so he didn't get as drunk. Jack would sit at the back of the train and share the liquor with the conductor. He was popular.

Jack used to say that he had never cut down a tree for firewood or bought any. He kept warm with fallen trees he found, wood scrap from his building, and coal he picked up.

The old house wasn't too big, with a potbelly stove on a huge piece of granite four feet square with two pieces behind it in a corner of his sitting room. Jack would get the stove's belly glowing red when he stoked it with coal. His kitchen area was a wing off to the side with a big cookstove that had been his mother's. Keeping the kitchen off the main house kept the house cooler in the summer.

Anything that might be considered trash was burned except bones. Bones were kept, no matter what kind, to be dried and crushed into bone meal fertilizer. Jack had a friend at Kunkel Forge who would put the bones on a machine that would crush them into a coarse powder to use in the garden. Fact is most anything organic like coffee grounds, tea bags, even urine, had a use.

When Jack would hear of someone wanting to build in the area, he always quietly did his own research on them to see if he wanted them in his area. If so, he would try and sell them one of his lots. Even better, sell them a lot and build them a house with as much scavenged wood as possible. When he did sell property, it was always through his good friend Henry Dean, Esquire, and justice of the peace. To Jack, he was Harry.

I actually knew Mr. Dean back in the 1960s. He was in his nineties and still practicing law in Boston, traveling by bus.

We were little kids and scared to death of old Mr. Dean. He lived on the top floor of another three-decker house in Readville built by Jack. We never saw lights on in the first or second floors, just on the third floor where he lived.

Next to the house was an old dilapidated building that we were sure was haunted. New kids moving into the neighborhood were initiated by going in and running back out. We always told them we had done it, too, which wasn't true. It may not have been haunted, but there were rats and bats.

Jack loved to study from books, and one that he spent much time reading was *Household and Farmers' Cyclopedia*. Written in 1878, it was advertised to have "one hundred thousand facts" for reference. I have Jack's well-worn copy. Inside the front cover is printed "John M. McDonough."

There is a section that is bookmarked for "Curing, Storing and Preserving," starting with apples and ending with wine making, with everything in between, like meats and fish.

This is what Jack did, learning to make things work without much help or cash money. Utilities at the time were all wood, kerosene, and candles. This wasn't a difficult life. There was a comfortable outhouse, fresh well water was plentiful, and Jack actually had it pretty good. He was able to grow food, was skilled at woodworking, and could forage for meats and other useful things, having done so his entire life.

Jack had a passion for a good, comfortable hat. Almost everyone wore a hat at that time, men and women. He had a black man who made his hats. This man lived on one of the islands in Boston Harbor. His name was Walter, and he had come from an island down in the Caribbean. He had learned to weave hats as a child, and he found that the reeds growing in the meadow made good summer hats.

Walter worked at the rum factory down by Sprague Street, but he put his hats on consignment at Park Clothing Store in Cleary Square. Esta's Hattery was just across River Street, but they wouldn't carry his hats because he was a Negro.

Jack was hauling some lumber back to Readville when he came across Walter walking along Hyde Park Avenue and gave him a ride to the train station. Walter was an odd guy for this area, with a strange accent that was very hard to understand. Walter had sold a hat to Jack a year ago, and Jack found that Walter's straw hat for summer kept him cooler than the traditional ones he'd worn.

They shared a bottle of some very nice rum that Walter happened to have with him. Quality rum had been established back in colonial times, and as we know, Robert Bronsdon was very much involved in brokering loads of sugarcane from the West Indies. The first record of rum being produced in Boston was in 1664, just three years prior to Robert's arrival. Soon the cargo ships were sailing south with lumber and returning with quality rum and better yet, raw sugarcane.

Now as Boston grew, there were many tradesmen like lumbermen, coopers, blacksmiths, and men who had been distilling alcohol in England making whiskey. They learned to produce very high-quality rum, some of which was so good it could be used in place of gold for currency. Beer and ale were common and brewed at taverns that were required by law to serve grog.

But distilling was quite different, and there was an art to producing a clean, smooth liquor. Boston businesses with quality metal workers and coopers were able to build specialized distilling vessels and eventually made rum so good it could compete with whiskey.

They also found that distilleries could make other liquors as well. Once railroads were built, distilleries sprang up all along the rail line from Readville to downtown Boston, and the industry prospered.

Old Mr. Boston was still using the buildings near Sprague Street when I was young, and we could smell alcohol in the air when walking past. Old bottles from that company are very collectable today.

# CHAPTER 19

# Life in Readville and Beyond

EGGS CAME FRESH DAILY FROM chickens Jackie Bronsdon kept in the barn. Everyone had their chores. He had an area for them to roost and lay eggs, a very important and sustainable food. They were kept in a basket hanging in the kitchen, as eggs will keep for a week or more, longer in cooler weather.

When a hen became "broody" or motherly and began sitting on a nest of her eggs or those of other hens, these eggs would produce baby chicks that would start out eating cornmeal. As they grew, their diet consisted of some cracked corn and all the fresh water they desired. Most of their food came from scratching and pecking around the area. They had a regular routine, usually staying together for protection, but if one of the hens found a sumptuous grub, toad, or even a mouse, they'd try to hide from the group.

When the rooster, usually named Sunday, who was always watching his girls, took his count and noticed a missing hen, he would go looking for safety. If he found she was eating something special before she could finish the tidbit would be his for the taking. He was the boss.

When a predator came around, it was one of Sunday's jobs to first alert the hens and then try to fend off the problem animal. If Sunday had a problem, Yippee, Jackie's dog, was never far away, and that howling bark let everyone know something was wrong. Yippee was a great dog, and when his space was invaded, he was strong and able. There were many roosters by the name of Sunday, as they would one day be eaten on a special Sunday for dinner, with bread stuffing, gravy, and cranberry sauce.

Annie always had cranberry sauce in the cellar, put up in jars every year. There were cranberries available in the fall before Thanksgiving, shipped up from cranberry bogs down in Carver, south of Boston near Plymouth. They came on the train in wood boxes with the grower's name on the sides. A box was about forty pounds. They were perfectly fresh, hard, shiny, and a nice crimson red. Most of them went into sauces, breads, and relishes, but they actually kept all winter in the root cellar. Mamie liked to chew on them raw when she felt a cold coming on. She was told the berries had lots of vitamin C.

There was need for only one rooster at a time, and he was responsible for fertilizing the eggs to make sure there were always new chicks coming along. Soon after they hatched as chicks, Jackie could tell a rooster from a hen. He began to segregate the young roosters and fed them raw oats, high-protein grain, to fatten them up; eight-week-old roosters made great fried chicken.

Mamie actually taught Jackie how to tell the sex of a chicken. It was something that had to be learned by looking close. They would turn a newborn chick upside down and brush back some fuzzy feathers, looking for the vent. With a slight squeeze, the vent opened enough to look for a tiny bump that meant a rooster. Mamie had learned this from her mother when she was just a young girl. Neither Annie nor Billy could see it, but they didn't do it often enough. Then the roosters could be put in a confined cage and fed differently to fatten them up nicely.

There was an area in the basement adjacent to the root cellar with hooks in the ceiling. Jackie would take a burlap sack, cut a hole in the bottom corner and hang the sack with the chicken in it, its head hanging through the hole, to cut the throat and bleed it into a bucket. The chicken was dinner soon after. A roast chicken dinner was a great meal, and there were never leftovers.

The big old broody hens would cover a whole clutch of eggs and set on them until they hatched. These old hens didn't lay eggs anymore but made a soup or stew during the winter. Chicken and dumplings was a specialty of Annie's, and it was Billy's favorite on a cold winter night.

Being in the freight business had many advantages. Well known around Boston, Billy was able to barter with some of his customers in and around Faneuil Hall. This structure was originally built in 1742 with funding from

Peter Faneuil, a wealthy Bostonian. He was responsible for directing local artist Deacon Shem Drowne to make the grasshopper weathervane. Four feet long, weighing eighty pounds, and made of gilded copper, it is still up there today. Peter Faneuil knew that the Royal Exchange in London was adorned with a great grasshopper, which became known as a symbol of trade. The grasshopper on Faneuil Hall could be seen all over Boston Harbor to indicate a place of commerce as well. Faneuil Hall was built as a meeting place, where many could gather to hear men like Samuel Adams speak to rally the colonists.

Shem Drowne was born in Maine on December 4, 1683. He moved south to Boston in 1699 to escape King William's War, also known as the Second Indian War.

After coming to Boston, he married Katherine Clark on September 18, 1712, and soon made America's first weathervane. The piece was a gilded archer for the royal governor's house in 1716.

The original hall was destroyed by fire in 1761, rebuilt in 1762, and became a theater for many years. As time went by, the building became a marketplace, beginning in the basement, which was all stone and very deep, dark, and cool. It was ideal at the time as a place for perishables such as meats and cheese. Though rats were a constant problem, being so close to the waterfront the rodents were being coming with cargo on ships from England.

Billy and Murch had a specially made wagon that could carry plenty of ice, and with a team of four horses, they delivered meat around the greater Boston area. Billy would barter with the merchants for their meats and cheeses by discounting their freight bills, not spending cash.

Some residents of the city anticipated when fishing boats were due to arrive in Boston Harbor, docking to unload their catch at the Atlantic Avenue fish pier. They'd wait while the ship was unloaded, and the crew would toss beautiful whole codfish to whoever wanted some. The fish were so plentiful they would fill the hold and pile more on deck. These were daily catch to be unloaded and processed the same day.

Billy was friendly with a particular captain, and there would be a box with fish on ice for him, normally every Thursday. He would return to Readville and divide the fish with everybody working for him. Mamie loved fresh fish rolled in cornmeal and fried in bacon fat.

Fishing was an important and prosperous industry in Boston, Gloucester, and New Bedford. Fresh fish needed to be iced and consumed within a day or two, but dried, salted, pickled, or smoked fish were shipped out of Boston to many parts of the country. Dried salt cod could be kept in a wooden box or hung in the kitchen without refrigeration indefinitely.

As fast as the fish were unloaded, they were moved into the processing room, which had long benches lined up in rows where men in aprons and boots, wielding razor-sharp knives, cleaned the catch. Everything was used, and every man had a particular job for cutting. A "wing of cod" was a whole cod gutted, with the head removed, and butterfly cut to flatten it for drying. After the cod's head was removed, another fishmonger would remove the "cheeks"; these were a delicacy, and the ship's captain and fish house owner had first choice. Once they were taken care of, there were plenty to divide up among the cutters. The rest of the head would be sent over to the Union Oyster House or Durgin Park for making chowder. Even the livers were saved and processed into cod liver oil.

Before drying, the fish would go to the salt room and be completely covered with salt and left for several hours. The fish had to be completely salted, or bacteria could grow. The piers along the waterfront had massive racks set up high for drying the fish with a roof to keep rain off. The walls were open slatted to allow air to flow through.

Smoking was another way of preserving fish, and there were big brick rooms with hooks hanging to attach the fish. A smoky fire would be kept tended for forty-eight hours until the smoking was done. This fish would keep longer than fresh, but time was limited depending on storage.

The New York, New Haven, and Hartford railroad operated from the mid-nineteenth century, and in the 1890s built a locomotive shop near Sprague's Pond. This was a massive building with huge doors that opened to bring trains inside for repairs or to build a locomotive from the rail up.

Just across the tracks was Frank Kunkel & Son Forge, established in 1883, which could make any part the trainmen needed. Readville was a very busy village and would continue to grow through the years. Freight yard employees worked overnight arranging trains on different tracks. The sound of trains rolling and clattering when hitching to one another was something residents got used to. I remember Mamie saying how much she missed those sounds when she was away.

There was a general store called J. A. Crowley's just across from the rail station. And Brewers Coffee House, which was only open in the mornings, was by the corner of Prescott Street. A saloon called Cap's was about fifty yards from the freight yard, and it was all within Wolcott Square, which was named for former Governor Roger Wolcott, a resident of Readville. The few who lived here tried to keep it to themselves. Other than the train yard, it was quiet and peaceful place.

Not at all like urban Boston.

Readville was as far south to southwest from the city as you could get, but to get downtown from the Bronsdon Livery on Hamilton Street, you could go in one of two directions: up through Milton into Quincy and then to Boston, or the most direct route, up Blue Hill Avenue into Mattapan, which led right into Roxbury and the downtown areas. It was still an all-day trip.

Trash was a problem in some areas, but burning barrels were common, and that was a way of cleaning up. Billy had several barrels around his property where he would burn trash and debris during winter months. It gave his men places to warm up a little while working outdoors and kept his place respectable.

There were men on wagons who collected things like rags, and a local pig farmer was always looking for garbage in the more densely populated areas.

There is a central section within the city of Boston originating in the West Roxbury/Hyde Park area called Turtle Pond. This pond is a shallow area leading to swampy and wooded sections with an outlet called Stony Brook. It then becomes the Stony Brook Reservation, which is now protected. The brook runs from Hyde Park, Roslindale, Jamaica Plain, and Roxbury before emptying into the Charles River at the Atlantic Ocean. From the early days, it was the headwater for a sewer system used for factory waste at mills.

After the Boston and Providence Railroad was established along Stony Brook and many breweries and distilleries were built, this brook would now become the drainage pits and eventually covered underground sewers in the elite Fenway area of Boston. It was later dredged for a retention pond and a green area in the city designed, planned, and built by Fredrick Law Olmstead. Today, it is known as the Emerald Necklace.

Olmstead was the father of American architecture. He was born in Hartford, Connecticut, on April 26, 1822, and died in Belmont, Massachusetts, on August 28, 1903. His accomplishments are still seen and used by thousands today.

There were burning barrels around places like Wolcott Square, and in the winter, there would be a man roasting chestnuts to sell fresh and hot. The fires were convenient for warming up quickly while walking. Put some hot chestnuts in your coat pockets, and they helped keep you warm while you were walking or riding the train and eating them. They were sweet and tasty, and most conductors didn't mind chestnuts or peanuts so long as people kept the mess to a minimum.

It was the conductor's job to keep his cars reasonably clean. There was a crew that started at two o'clock in the morning, when the cars were thoroughly cleaned. This work was done by the same men who were porters, janitors, and other menial workers. They were normally black men, and they were happy to have the jobs. One benefit of the job was free train travel. The benefit worked in a number of ways. It gave the men transportation without cost; that way they could live in poor Boston neighborhoods and walk to the train to get to work. They could use the trains for themselves as they wanted, but these men worked twelve to sixteen hours a day and at least six days a week; some worked seven days.

On the walk to the train station from Wolcott Square, there is a massive tunnel built of huge granite blocks that had been quarried in Quincy and moved overland by the Granite Railway Company down to the lower mills area where the Bakers chocolate factory was located. From there the huge stones were hauled by sleds pulled by oxen teams. The oxen could pull heavier loads for longer periods, and they were driven by men called teamsters. Oxen were steers that were castrated young to make them more docile and easier to control while working, and they would grow to more than a thousand pounds.

Once the teams brought the material to Readville, the massive granite stones were handled by master masons. The work was very impressive and drew many spectators, especially when the men put the most important piece in place: the keystone. Stone construction has been used since ancient times, dating back to early Rome, the keystone was the most critical piece of the design. If this was not done properly, the entire arch would fail. First, a strong, wood-frame structure was built in a shape that was determined with many factors in mind: length, width, height, and many angles. Just as important was the weight of the stones that would be used in construction. It was also necessary to know how much weight the arch would be supporting.

Back in the late nineteenth century, there were as many as two hundred trains traveling through Readville per day—big iron locomotives carrying tons of coal for fuel and pulling twenty or more freight or passenger cars. Growing up in Readville, going to sleep at night, I could at times hear the freight yard being arranged for the next day's shipping. I found the sound relaxing and comforting at three in the morning.

The skewed stone arch bridge was designed to carry nine tracks and span Hyde Park Avenue, separating the Wolcott Square section of Readville from the rest of Boston and what would become "the other side of Readville." The most technically challenging stone bridge in Boston, its base is pilings driven almost twelve feet into quicksand. Next, a fleet of carpenters and laborers built the massive wood structure that would become the mold for the stonework. Once this was built, the masons took over, working with massive pieces of granite brought in from Quincy. Experienced masons used the wood arch to make patterns to develop the angles required to make each piece fit with very close tolerance, even by today's standards. During the stonework, two vertical arched stairways leading up to the tracks were built inside, which added to the challenges of the building process. The center or "crown" was built fifteen feet from street level. It was then waterproofed with several layers of tar paper and tar. Next, a thick structural layer of concrete tar was poured over the entire area.

Eventually tracks were laid, and buildings, both stone and wood, were constructed for many uses all along both sides, with still more tracks at street level leaving Wolcott Square, creating the freight yard and repair area for taking trains off the main lines.

Getting foot traffic from side to side meant another tunnel under many more tracks. It was built of granite blocks twelve feet wide and just eight feet high, with a stairway at each end. The stairs went down about twelve feet to a stone chamber one hundred and fifty feet long under the train tracks. This was much deeper in the center, as its construction was based on the same arch design as the tunnel.

Readville Depot became a very important part of the growth and defense of the United States of America. It is still a very active and important train station used by Amtrak and the Massachusetts Bay Transportation Authority connecting travelers from Readville to downtown Boston or as far away as San Francisco.

The new station was being constructed right around the same time in 1832 that a young artist sailing back to the United States had an idea based on electricity. Samuel Morse, while discussing the idea, actually talked himself through what would become the first single-wire communications device. Until then, the world had relied on carrier pigeons and pony express for rural mail, and trains were now connecting many cities across the country. By 1838 Morse had obtained a patent, and in 1843 he was given a $30,000 grant from Congress to develop this system. Railroads would make for a good start to running the wires to send the current and produce what would be known as Morse code. The trains made it easier to send men and material to remote areas to install poles and string the wire and they had a clear direction along the tracks. Everything from news and train delays to weather and finances could now be communicated hundreds and eventually thousands of miles.

The telegraph office at the rail yard was a common place to find hackney drivers either waiting for a train or a fare. There was a standard practice of pulling through the station to see if there was anyone waiting for a carriage. Mamie enjoyed sitting in the office listening to the tap-tap-tap of the different sequences.

There was another telegraph office that was part of the post office, and W. D. Chisolm did the telegraph job part time; he was the postal carrier as well. Walter Douglas Chisolm and Mamie were good friends—he was Wally to Mamie—and he was giving her lessons on the Morse system.

She was also friendly with the night clerk at the rail station. He worked a twelve-hour shift, six days a week. There was no mail to be sorted on Sunday, so he had the day off. On the other days, he worked from four in the afternoon to four in the morning, and he was responsible for the telegraphs from eight in the evening to two in the morning or when his mail car arrived. When there was something urgent, an SOS would be sent and answered right away by anyone hearing the call for help. Three dots, three dashes, and three dots again became the international emergency code in 1906, becoming effective July 1, 1908.

Mr. Chisolm was giving Mamie lessons, and she liked to sit in his office with a pad of paper and pencil and write down what she heard. Then she'd read it back to the clerk on duty, who was amazed at how well she did. After all, this too was considered man's work. Whenever someone reminded Mamie that something was "man's work," she would ask if they put their pants on differently than she did or if one just perceived that they might. She never waited for an answer.

# CHAPTER 20

# Annie

ANNIE WAS UP IN HER new house in the sky, as everyone referred to it, when Mamie got back from visiting Jack. She tended to stay there for long periods because of the stairs she had to climb.

Annie J. Bronsdon

The view from her rocking chair on the porch was spectacular. The house behind her is 19 Hamilton Street, the Bronsdon Express office.

When Mamie came in, Annie was just in the middle of making supper. It was almost five o'clock. Billy would be coming home to eat anytime now, so Annie set a place for Mamie, too. You could set your watch by him, and when Mamie saw Billy coming up from the direction of the firehouse, she went over to a window to call down for him to get a couple of cukes and tomatoes from the porch to have with supper. She asked Annie if she had any cider vinegar. After thinking a minute, Annie said it was still over at 19, as she referred to the old house. Just then, Billy came through the door.

"OK, salt will have to do," said Annie, "unless someone wants to run over to the old pantry."

She hadn't been in her new home very long and was still trying to stock her shelves, so she was keeping a list. Someone would drop the list off at Crowley's store, and Joe Mahoney would send a delivery boy with her goods. This was all dry goods, nonperishables like coffee, sugar, salt, flour, and vinegar that were kept on the shelf, but staples that were used regularly. More often, though, Billy or Murch would be in downtown Boston where there was a fine coffee roasting company at 291 Atlantic Avenue on the corner of India Street across from Lewis Wharf. Everywhere in the area, you could tell by the smell when they were roasting beans; it was wonderful. When the air was thick with salty brine and the warm smell of fresh coffee, "It must be what heaven might smell like," Billy would say. Their coffee was called LA Touraine. Adriel U. Bird was president of the W. S. Quinby Company, distributer of the French product.

The old house had a huge root cellar that would stay cool even in August. Down there was a big block of ice, usually cut from Sprague's Pond just over the railroad tracks, which Annie could see from her new nest in the winter, when there were no leaves on the trees. The block of ice would be covered in sawdust and a blanket of burlap and would keep for a long time. Now living up on the third floor, Annie had an icebox that needed to be stocked two or three times a week in the summer. Winter was different; she just used her front or rear porch for an icebox.

The ice delivery man, Tut Coughlin, was never very pleasant, and now having to lug fifty-pound blocks of ice to the third floor in the summer, he hated this delivery. Annie knew that and would scold him, saying, "I don't know how you do anything drinking that rotgut whiskey, and it's not even noon." Tut was almost always drunk and kept a bottle of cheap whiskey on ice. Later in the day, he'd be at the saloon where all the railmen went after work. Then, at about six o'clock nightly, the commotion would start, with Tut's wife, Milly, heading down the avenue to herd him home. They lived about halfway between the rail yard and the racetrack. Milly wasn't very big, but the frying pan she would hit him with all the way home made up for her small size.

Milk and cream were delivered by Mr. Moran and his wife, Elsey. They had a dozen or so milk cows and delivered twice a week. The milk was so creamy you could stand a spoon straight up in it. That was just what Annie needed, fresh heavy cream to make her own butter.

This was a time when the old root cellar was perfect. She kept a big granite slab by the block of ice, and the day before making butter, she'd have Billy lay the ice block on top of the stone to chill it. Her granite slab had been used by her mother. Annie's father, James, had a friend at a Quincy monument company make it smooth as glass, the same as a headstone—in fact, it would have been a headstone had James not wanted it.

When the cream was delivered, Elsey knew enough to deliver it to 19 in the box by the bulkhead going down to the cellar. When it was extremely cold out, she would make sure it was left just inside the door.

Annie would have four quarts of cream delivered once a week. Those four quarts would produce three pounds of butter and one quart of buttermilk. The first thing to do was to let the cream get good and chilled. Having made butter almost all her life, she could pretty much tell by touch when it was about right. Her mother always said that cold cream turns to butter more easily than warm; warm will still make butter, but it takes more work.

The butter churns were replaced every year for cleanliness. Annie used a container made of wood with two sets of paddles. The device was hand cranked like a coffee grinder. As the paddles moved like a hand mixer through the liquid, they quickly broke the cream up by mixing it with air. This allowed her to make the butter faster than by simply agitating the cream. Once the cream broke down and became a large mass of solidified milk fat, it needed to be worked and salted.

Next, with the stone slab nice and chilled, the now semisolid butter was scooped out onto the slab, and Annie would form it with wood paddles that were older than she was. The mass would give up a bit more liquid as it was worked and pressed with the hand paddles. While paddling the butter, she would add salt to it, mixing and adding a little at a time. She knew the amount and had it premeasured. The salt would add flavor to the butter and help preserve it a little longer. Being very fresh and salted, it did not need refrigeration in cool weather. It didn't last long anyway.

Later, she would have soda crackers slathered with fresh butter and a cup of tea. Every day at two o'clock in the afternoon, this was her ritual. Whenever Mamie was anywhere close at two o'clock, she knew to stop and see Annie. They grew up with this daily as young girls, when their mother, Bridget, would have the same afternoon tea. This was an Irish tradition brought from the motherland.

Annie and Mamie both loved to read and do crossword puzzles, and a large part of the sisters' education was reading aloud around the house. That way, James and Bridget could get used to hearing words spoken without too much brogue to learn proper American dialect. When one girl was speaking, the other was to write down what was being said, and Bridget was looking for good penmanship. Being able to write was very important, but the ability to write in cursive was thought to be a sign of great intelligence. Legible cursive can be a thing of beauty and shows the talent and ability of the writer.

Bridget would have the girls write letters for her to send back to Ireland, which gave them some background on where she and James had come from. Both Annie and Mary hoped to see this country one day, though they never would.

One thing they had both enjoyed ever since they were young girls was going to the haberdashery; it was so much fun. It had all the little items needed for sewing or knitting; spoons, knives, and other utensils; and many other little items. They shopped and enjoyed an hour or so browsing the shelves.

Now Mamie was driving, so they could go to any shops they wanted to—what a great freedom for the day. Mamie was very good with money and didn't spend very much at all, but Annie never had any cash or the need for it, as Billy took care of all that. When she was going off with Mamie, though, Billy always gave her some money. That was normal, and Annie would spend every penny, but she brought something home for everybody else as well.

There was a favorite thing she almost always bought for Billy: a bismarck. This was the German name for a fresh cake like a donut but softer, split down the middle with raspberry jelly and a whipped, sweet-cream filling. The women had a hard time getting them home without eating them. Billy savored his prize every time. The bismarck, or *bismarcken* in German, was named for Chancellor Otto von Bismarck during the mid-1800s and was brought to the United States by German immigrants during the early 1900s.

# CHAPTER 21

# Avis Bronsdon and the Getchell's

AVIS DELIA BRONSDON, BILLY AND Annie's daughter, was seeing a young German man. His name was Ernest Rau, and he went by Ernie.

Germans were known to be strong and hardworking people. Ernie was strong, not tall but a large-built and good-looking man. He took on various jobs and did very well at whatever he put his mind to. He had a green thumb like Jack, though he was not as accomplished as Jack. But he was much younger than Jack and didn't have a place of his own to grow much. His mother taught him much about the way of the land and how to make ends meet on very little.

While Mamie was driving her patrons, they would regularly have her stop to pick up at businesses along their route. A café in Canton, just across the Milton line by the foot of Blue Hill, was famous for its baked goods, especially pies. The crusts were light, flaky, sweet, salty, and savory; they just melted in your mouth. Mamie, who loved to cook, would find time to hang around watching the baker ply her skill. She learned that the most important thing about the crust was the temperature of the lard and the humidity in the air. The woman who did the baking was a domestic baker and very good at her trade. She seemed to know things that many missed. She had been born to a Wampanoag woman and was very proud of her heritage, having been taught a primitive way of life from a very early age.

Edith Estella Getchell was actually Ada Estella Getchell, born on July 21, 1874, in Acushnet, Massachusetts, fifty miles south-southwest of Boston. The ocean nearby, and the area littered with ponds teeming with fish and forestland with exceptional hunting. Edith learned much from her peers and the surrounding area. She could fish and gather foods like mushrooms, roots, and berries from the forest floor, and she learned to cook using open flame and hot coals.

Edith's mother, Mary, was of Native American descent, born in Maine on October 13, 1845. She later moved back to Acushnet, Massachusetts having come from this Wampanoag clan. She had taken a white man as her husband. This was not a popular thing to do for either race, but her mother was a respected woman, and her people accepted them both.

Edith enjoyed her time living in Acushnet, but with winter wind, snow, and ice, food became scarce there.

Acushnet, first settled in 1659, takes its name from the town's river Acushnet, pronounced *Cushnea* in Wampanoag, which means "quiet resting place near water." The well-known author Herman Melville signed onto the whaling ship *Acushnet* in 1841, eventually writing the classic adventure *Moby-Dick*.

James A. Getchell, Edith's father, was born on November 21, 1832, in Salem, Massachusetts, to a farming family. He enlisted in the Union army on February 24, 1862, and was assigned to the Massachusetts First Heavy Artillery Regiment, Company D. He was wounded but survived and was mustered out in 1865 after the war's end. He returned to Salem and became an oyster dealer, later meeting and marrying Mary while in Maine buying his goods, then residing in the Boston area. They eventually moved to 53 Trull Street in the city of Somerville.

Because he was injured in the war, James could not do the heavy work needed on the farm. Having lived in Salem with the ocean nearby, he was able to establish himself as a shellfish dealer with connections to the sea captains he knew. He didn't work a pushcart, as was common at the time; there were men selling everything from shellfish to meats to vegetables and even household goods. James was bringing in shipments of oysters from Maine and distributing them to shops, taverns, and pushcarts. They were big and sweet, from a place that James would not reveal, even to his friends. The oysters were from the mouth of a river in Damariscotta that flows into Salt Bay; this area is all tidal but is protected from open ocean at Pemaquid Point and up into the Damariscotta River. The cold, clear water is brackish, salt and fresh water mixed, where the best oysters are found, with a nice, firm but juicy texture and sweet, salty, and smooth taste.

There were times that James would sail up to Maine to keep up his dealings with the suppliers. The oysters would come in wooden boxes packed with ice, covered with wet burlap and a layer of sawdust. The lakes in Maine were a great source for winter ice harvesting.

The area around Salt Bay shows evidence of shellfish being consumed as many as twelve thousand years ago. The natives left what are called middens or scrap piles of clam, oyster, and other shells. Some middens were many feet thick—an amazing sight to behold—until it was found that the shells, when ground up and added to garden soil, improved it greatly. Thousands of pounds were taken to be ground and sold for fertilizer.

Some shellfish mongers who didn't normally buy from James at times when catches were plentiful were getting shellfish from the southern waters of Massachusetts and Cape Cod in the colder months.

During the summer, oysters sit in estuaries, and the water gets much warmer. This causes the oysters to reproduce, and the meat gets soft and not very tasty. There were some who thought eating oysters at these times would make you sick, so they were only harvested during months that end in *r*. Most suppliers only had oysters four months a year, from September through December.

James could get another four months of harvest from the cold, flowing water of the Damariscotta River. And the mineral-rich sediment that flowed over the oysters kept them firm and sweet year round. He kept the Boston area supplied and made good profits. These are still some of the best oysters I have ever tasted.

## CHAPTER 22

# Hoboes and Freddy

⁓

READVILLE, WITH ITS LOCATION, RAIL yard, and depot, had a tremendous amount of train traffic. The locomotive repair shop and huge freight yard were used as a holding area for freight cars coming into Boston or going to other parts of the country. Outgoing freight was loaded in the yard twenty-four hours a day. Depending on where the freight was going, the men would swap around train cars, lining them up for shipping. Factories and mills along the tracks had spurs to move freight cars over to loading docks for great savings and convenience. The rail yard played an important role in transporting large numbers of troops from Camp Meigs during the Civil War as well.

In the time following the war, train service expanded to the west, and freight hopping became a common form of transportation for many drifters and immigrants. They became known as hoboes. They moved almost daily, stopping to camp along the way and try to find a group to eat and sleep with at night for protection. Some were just boys.

The Bronsdon Brothers freight business was a mere quarter mile from the depot and just 150 feet off the rear of his property to the railroad tracks adjacent to the depot. The barn that the horses were stabled in became a frequent stop for many a hobo. The well water was clean and cold, and the barn had a nice hayloft that was comfortable year round. Billy was usually willing to give the men a place to stay, but they had to ask. The main reason they had to ask Billy himself was that he was good at reading their faces and language, and he wanted to know who was on his property. If you didn't pass muster with Billy, it was time to find another place to stay, but not many were refused.

He would then take all matches, cigars, pipes, and tobacco until morning to avoid smoking and a fire. A real bonus was that he always gave them a bowl of something that Annie had on the stove with bread and coffee. Some got to know this and planned the stop.

There was a sign by the street that said "Vagrants and drunks keep out," and that was enforced. The difference between a vagrant and a hobo was that a vagrant was just a lazy bum trying to get something for nothing. A hobo was a man down on his luck but trying to find some work.

Billy kept a train schedule on the wall by the barn door, and some of the regulars got to know how to read it and determine which train would be on which track and the departure and arrival times. Billy kept this for his drivers, but he had no problem with the drifters using the information. Some of the more experienced riders could use Billy's schedule to be on a freight car before it started moving; it was much safer that way. The only drawback was the occasional nonscheduled change, which could result in a long, unexpected trip.

First, the hitchhikers had to figure out which trains were going in the direction that they wanted to go. Then they would have to catch a train on the fly, meaning they had to grab onto a moving train and pull themselves aboard. But they had to do this when the yard crew was changing; otherwise, they would be thrown off and at times beaten because of the damage caused by some bad apples. The experienced men knew the best times, and others would follow when allowed, but they were on their own.

From the end of the nineteenth century well into the twentieth century, there were tremendous numbers of orphaned children. Some had one parent who couldn't care for them or who abused and neglected them, while others were deemed incorrigible and likely headed for troubled lives. At times they became homeless as young as five or six years old and had to try to survive on their own.

There was one young boy who came through whom Billy helped, a nice kid with thin build. His name was Fredrick A. Stewart, or Freddy. He was just a young boy when he tried to steal Billy's horse. Here was an eight-year-old boy who was hungry enough to try something so dumb. Billy couldn't be mad; that was his demeanor.

That day, he handed the boy a biscuit he had with him, and the kid devoured it. Then Billy asked where he lived, but there was no answer. Billy asked if he had any family, and the boy replied, "No, sir." Billy told him to get up on the carriage, and they drove home. He really took a liking to this young kid. And Freddy stayed on awhile.

Freddy would chop wood, clean stalls, and feed and water the horses. Billy kept him busy. Soon Freddy was coming into the house for regular meals, and Annie took a liking to him as well. He insisted on washing the dishes for her.

After he had stayed with them for a while, Billy and Annie adopted Freddy, and he became their son. Everybody was happy, and the young man had a second chance.

Mamie was always helpful with anything anybody needed, and as she watched Freddy learn to bridle horses, she would stop him and show him a better way. Freddy listened and appreciated Mamie's help. He became good at his job.

Mamie had an idea.

She knew that Billy was doing a daily carriage run to Hyde Park and back at a time of day when all his drivers were busy. With his many other jobs, this was stretching him thin. Mamie had been quietly teaching Freddy to drive her carriage and decided to suggest that Freddy make that run to help Billy.

Mamie brought this up to Billy, and he smiled at her with a surprised look. She told him that she'd been teaching Freddy to drive, and he was a natural. Billy fully respected Mamie's opinion, and she was well spoken for a woman of this day and age. He called Freddy over and told him to climb up on his carriage and take it up and down Hamilton Street so he could watch.

Freddy, with a big smile, leaped up into the carriage in one motion, and settled himself into the seat. He took the reins, and with a shake and a whistle, the horse and carriage pulled away. He had been tending to the horse, and Silver was comfortable with him. They strode off nicely; up and down Hamilton Street twice they went. When Billy called him back over, he reached up to shake Freddy's hand and congratulate him.

Billy then said, "At two-thirty this afternoon, you make the run to Hyde Park with me, and we'll see how that goes."

Freddy looked at Mamie, and she smiled with a wink and headed off on a carriage run.

He and Mamie were friendly, and she treated him just like she was his aunt. He had supper with her many times, especially when she told him during the day that she was planning to make a pigeon pie that night. That had become his favorite meal, and Mamie made a crust that was amazing. Edith would have been proud.

Another thing Mamie enjoyed doing was making homemade cider donuts, because she liked to see people happy. She only made them in fall, when the apples were ripe. She would go to an orchard up in Milton and do "pickups" of the apples that had fallen off the trees. These were sold for a penny a pound if you picked them up yourself. The orchard had a cider press for pressing the juice out of the apples. Hard apple cider was widely consumed.

Mamie would come home with two or three gallons of sweet cider. Much of the fruit she picked up was in good shape, and she saved some for eating. Any apples that had started rotting became apple butter: rendered-down apples sweetened with some sugar and Mamie's special seasoning, salt, which brought out the apple flavor. On toasted wheat bread, this was her fall and winter favorite.

The owner of the orchard saved all the mashed apple bits and distilled applejack (hard cider) as well. Jack loved the stuff; Mamie knew that but didn't buy it for him. She refused to buy alcohol or tobacco for anyone.

When one of the drifters suggested that the loft in the barn where the men bedded down smelled awful, without looking up, Mamie responded, "Well, with four men badly in need of a bath, it's no wonder. But as long as the horses don't mind, you'll be fine."

Some of the hoboes traveling and looking for work were known as pickers. They traveled to farms; it was good work but seasonal. Some fruit and vegetable farmers in the area knew the Bronsdon's had pickers coming through at times and advertised through Billy. When these men showed up at the barn looking for work, Billy would have a list posted on the wall near his schedule.

Mamie had friends who were farmers and hired pickers from time to time as well. She was very selective and didn't list these jobs on the board. She asked

Billy for his opinion before helping get work for anyone she didn't know very well. Mamie wasn't a boss, but she had the respect of her peers and everyone who knew her.

Billy had other jobs for the men as well. His regular crew was always busy, and everyone in town was required to do roadwork, filling holes or grading sections. There was a tax on anyone who did not or could not do this work. The tax raised money to pay someone else to do the work.

The Bronsdon's homes and business were on Hamilton Street, and Billy was proud of what he and Murch had built. They wanted the area to be presentable and the street to be a smooth ride. This was one of the chores that he had his boarders take care of for him, and in return they had a place to sleep in the barn and a good meal.

The residents of Hamilton Street at the time formed a committee, calling it the Hamilton Street Preservation Committee. Tree lined Hamilton Street had maples on both sides, starting at the firehouse and church and running all the way down past the Meigs Monument to the edge of the racetrack. The area that was formerly the camp had huge granite cannon mounts and benches as a memorial for celebrations on the Fourth of July. This was appropriate for Camp Meigs, where so many men trained for battle and became part of the greatest loss of life in any American conflict.

There were Fourth of July festivities at Meigs. Back in the 1960s when I was growing up, *Cappy's Tavern*, the local tap in Wolcott Square, Ray *Cappy* Capobiano sponsored the event. There were games, races, ice cream, and "tonic" the term used for "soda" in the Boston area. Cappy's is still there run by *Raymond Jr.* and very much upscaled since the 1970s.

Back in the early 1960s there were probably a hundred kids with parents and Cap would have an open-top trailer full of cans of beer on ice for the men. They had a children's dress-up parade, and in 1963 after the Cuban missile crisis, my mother dressed me up to look like Castro, beard and all. Riding my red tractor with a sign that said "No blockade," I won first prize.

# CHAPTER 23

# The Rau Connection

EDITH'S PARENTS MOVED TO THE Boston area near Somerville so that her father could be closer to more outlets for his oysters. Edith was not happy there; she enjoyed nature, with birds singing and the smell of the forest, and longed to be back in the country air. She enjoyed going to Acushnet every summer for her education on the natives' way of life.

On May 6, 1894, Edith was in Boston with her father picking up some freight for a customer. While she was waiting in the wagon, a commotion began on the other side of Tremont Street. A significant amount of smoke was coming around the corner from Cabot Street, people were running to and fro, and then there were flames. Her horse was becoming spooked.

She was trying to control the horse when a young man came over and asked if she needed help. Edith could not understand him with his strong accent; seeing her puzzled look, he jumped up onto the seat and removed them from the area quickly.

The fire was still growing, and it soon engulfed the entire perimeter of Tremont and Cabot Streets. This was the Great Roxbury Fire of 1894 that burned the Boston baseball grounds while the Boston Bean Eaters were playing the Baltimore Orioles.

Edith's father, James, was struck with fear upon not finding his daughter where he'd left her and began looking for her frantically. Then he heard her whistle for him. Edith had a very shrill and distinct whistle. Relieved but shaken, Edith told her father of the man's help, and they thanked him as he shyly smiled.

James asked his name, and with a German accent, he said his name was George Rau. James thanked him again and invited him to come for dinner to repay his help. He happily accepted, and James told him where they lived and to come around five o'clock.

He arrived about ten minutes early with a package in hand, which he gave to James. It was German sausage that he had made while working at Jacob Wurth, a German restaurant on Stuart Street that had been operating since 1868. He suggested they simmer it in beer. Then he handed James a small container of mustard that he said was "good with the bratwurst."

James, a bit confused, asked, "You said it is good and the worst?"

Then George explained that the German word for sausage is *wurst*.

George John Rau, born on November 21, 1873, in Württemberg, Germany, emigrated from the port of Bremen, in northwestern Germany, on the ship *Fulda*, arriving on Ellis Island, New York, on May 13, 1887. This was my great-grandfather.

He had a light complexion with blue eyes and brown hair, and at five feet six inches tall and 135 pounds, he was of average size. He spoke no English but was excited for a new life in America.

George was skilled as a machinist, but he needed to learn English. He carried a letter from his friend Karl Hagelman that instructed him what to do once he got to Boston: find the city marketplace with the huge copper grasshopper weathervane on top. Using the weathervane for direction, go northeast for one hundred yards to Jacob Wurth German Restaurant. Karl would be there.

George did find his friend and gained employment with Karl, and they had a place to stay in the attic area included. The goal now was to learn some English and become part of this new place.

George's father was Johann George Rau, born on July 11, 1809, also in Württemberg. His mother was Anna M. Kaiser, born in the same city on February 5, 1809. They were married there in 1832. Anna died on May 5, 1888, still in Württemberg, at the age of seventy-nine.

In this area of Germany, the name Rau is very common, even today. I would like to travel there someday to see what the area and the people are like and maybe discover a few relatives.

George learned English quickly. He was seeing Edith regularly and took many meals at her parents' home, where they all helped teach him his new language.

Now he was able to find employment working with machinery, and on November 28, 1895, George and Edith were married and would soon have a family of their own.

They lived with Edith's family in Somerville, and George found good work making parts and maintaining the machinery for a cotton gin company. He could take apart most any machine, find what had broken, make a new piece, and have it running again quickly.

On September 21, 1896, George and Edith had their first child, a son, Richard George Augustus Rau. Edith didn't want to raise her family in a city setting and longed for the country. They had saved some money, and George was able to buy a house with some land in Sharon, Massachusetts, about fifteen miles southwest of Boston, rural and quiet.

They had another son, Ernest Phillipe Rau, on May 13, 1898. This would be my grandfather. Two years later, Herbert Emanuel Rau was born on June 2, 1900.

The Rau clan was growing, and they needed more income to support them. There was a family of five girls living nearby, and their father owned a business in Canton. They would regularly come to ask if they could do chores for money or trade; food was always wanted. Edith would trade a pie for one of the girls to do chores for a day. After she had traded several pies, the girls' father came to meet her in person and wanted to know about her pie-baking skill. Her pies were simply the best he'd ever had. Even better than his mother's. He offered to hire her to come make pies for his business in Canton, about two miles away. The train depot at Sharon Heights was a short walk, and the Canton Depot was adjacent to his Blue Bird Café. He told Edith that he would have his daughters do the same chores they had been doing for a pie, caring for Edith's children, plus she could use the ingredients and oven at the café. He would pay her five cents for each pie she made for the Blue Bird on top of that.

She agreed to his terms, but said she could only work from ten o'clock in the morning until two in the afternoon. She could produce six pies a day with his ingredients at five cents each, one to pay his daughter to care for the children, plus one for herself to bring home for her family.

"Agreed."

Now Edith could make thirty cents a day and bring home a pie for supper at no cost. She soon found out that if she gave the conductor a slice of pie, she could save the two cents for her ride home.

Mamie didn't drive to Canton daily, but she had one patron Oak Ames who wanted to go to the Canton Depot to meet his wife on Tuesdays and Thursdays at one o'clock in the afternoon sharp. The afternoon train from Boston didn't pass through Readville until one thirty. Mamie was hired by Mr. Ames to drive him to Canton. The son of former Massachusetts Governor Oliver Ames of Easton. Oak ran the tool and shovel business owned by his family.

Mamie would hold off on lunch on those days to go and see Edith for a piece of pie. She would save Mamie a nice slice of her favorite, mincemeat, with ground meat, apples, currants, and raisins, seasoned with mace, clove, and nutmeg.

Mamie would go into the kitchen to watch, and Edith would explain the proper method for baking a perfect pie. Days when Mamie didn't have a patron for a while, she drove Edith home and enjoyed seeing her growing boys.

After a few years, the Rau clan began to grow again, and they had another boy, William Lenard Rau, born on January 2, 1903. Then Francis Henry Rau, born on February 28, 1905. Finally, after five boys, Edith gave birth to a girl, Mary Elizabeth Irene Rau, on August 4, 1907. Their last child was another boy, Charles Richard Rau, born on February 18, 1911.

# CHAPTER 24

# Dinner with Plans

MAMIE WAS NOW COMING AROUND to visit Jack regularly, and it was becoming common for them to have supper together two or three nights a week. He would see her in his travels during the day, and she would invite him for dinner if her schedule permitted. Her patrons still always came first, though she could easily explain that she'd stopped to care for a sick or hurt animal if she were late, which was never a problem, Mamie did what was best.

When she did invite Jack, he would say something like, "Do you care for pheasant?"

She responded, "Yes, but I already had something planned."

Mamie never passed up pheasant when offered; it was delicious. When Jack arrived, he had two nice pheasants for her. Now she realized that when Jack asked a question, he had a reason.

Mamie told him he shouldn't have bothered, but then confided that her horse had thrown a shoe and she'd been at the farrier's shop next to Kunkel's Forge. "I just got here minutes ago," she said. She was going get a smoked pork steak that one of her friends had told her to come by for, but she knew he'd be coming and didn't want him to think he'd been stood up. "I was going to clean a couple of pigeons, but now we go from squab to pheasant."

"We're society tonight," Jack said. "Mamie, my dear, that was no bother. They practically walk up to me," he added with a grin.

While she prepared supper, Jack went out and did what Jack did, weeded the garden. He also spread some pigeon droppings around as fertilizer, later telling Mamie that it was better than horse manure, as there were no weed seeds.

During supper, Mamie usually talked about her day's riders and news she'd picked up in her travels. Jack didn't see many people and most were not talkative, so it was interesting to hear Mamie speak. Sometimes she would go on so long that Jack wondered how she could breathe and talk so much.

He soon realized that Mamie was very good at putting up vegetables. Jack would let her know a week or so in advance what would be coming along to harvest. Mamie would let her friends know what Jack was harvesting and sell them produce as well.

She did her dishes, and Jack would sit and smoke a pipe. The pipe tobacco smell reminded her of her father when she was a child. Jack didn't normally drink in front of Mamie, so he went out to check on "things" regularly. But Jack smoked all the time in various ways. He started the day with a cigar. Then he'd hand roll cigarettes while drinking with friends, and smoked a pipe in the house.

There were times when Mamie heard a lot of political debate as she was driving. Some people would talk through their opinions while she drove, but she wasn't really listening.

Mamie had many female passengers; they felt most comfortable with her. There was one by the name of C. E. Guild. She was one of seven prominent women who organized women's suffrage. By 1915 they were well organized, with thirty-seven thousand members, headquartered on Boylston Street in Boston. Guild was always trying to talk Mamie into joining the organization to help, assuming that because she did the work of men, she would want to be treated the same. Not that Mamie disliked the idea, but it was very political, and she detested politics. She just smiled and never committed to anything.

Jack was not at all into politics. But he did vote, and he would tell Mamie that "they are all a bunch of crooks." Jack was so far removed from government, he just made sure his property tax was paid on time.

Jack always headed home once Mamie had finished the dishes, and she would sit in her rocker and sew a bit or read. When she started to doze off, she would go to bed. It might have been seven thirty, and depending on the season, it might have been light or dark outside, but four in the morning came quickly. With all the fresh air and the work of driving, she slept like a baby. Prince was asleep right there next to the bed.

Jack McDonough was acquiring lots of lumber. Building in Boston was booming, so the more lumber that came in on the railroad, the more that fell off the train cars. He was hustling to keep up, but he had a plan for that lumber, and it involved Mamie.

They were having supper together three and sometimes four nights a week and always Sunday dinner.

Mamie loved Jack's gardens. She told him many times that she could sit on his front step, which faced Blue Hill, and look at it forever.

The scenery changed with the seasons. When winter ended, the trees would come back to life in spring green, just light green at first. Then they seemed to magically transform to darker shades. Eventually, there was a green forest all around them, and it was beautiful. When fall rolled around, the colors were spectacular. The smell in the air was just grand.

One spring evening while having a supper of fresh asparagus on buttered toast, Jack asked her if she thought his company was becoming a burden. Mamie, taken aback, was speechless. Then she asked what she had done to make him think such a thing.

Jack said, "No, no, not like that. We seem to help each other regularly now, and maybe we might," he just blurted out, "get married?"

Mamie turned pink and then red and then flushed white, and Jack suggested he should leave. Mamie said, "No, no, no, you just threw me like a stallion. Why, where would we live? This place is barely big enough for me, and your place is even smaller."

Jack calmly said, "I have a plan. Mamie, you have some idea of the property I own, but I don't think you know the extent. I have been stockpiling lumber, and I have about what I need to build a big, beautiful house for you on my property. Now before you answer, we'll go down to Chester Street and let me show you."

The next afternoon, Mamie met Jack at his house, and he rolled out a paper drawing of the house he was planning. To Mamie this was just a sketch, and she had a hard time following what he was saying.

Jack took a few boards and a stepladder and had her follow him over toward Chester Street. About fifty feet off the street, he laid four boards end to end parallel to the street and stood the ladder to the right corner of the boards. Then he had Mamie come stand as high as she could on that ladder, and she did.

Jack asked, "What do you see?"

She laughed and said jokingly, "The roof of your house."

He asked her to look straight ahead. "What do you see?"

Mamie said, "My eyes go right to Blue Hill, then the meadow."

He said, "Yes, thank you. That will be the location of the kitchen sink with a big window. You'll be up higher still. It'll be a grand view looking out at Big Blue," he told her.

Then he moved two boards and placed them end to end from the corner where Mamie was. Then he walked almost to Chester Street, explaining, "This will be the front of the house. The house will be forty feet by twenty feet with an eight-foot-high basement and a root cellar as big as your sister's. There will be a full first floor and stairs to a second floor with bedrooms. The kitchen can be as big as you'd like."

Just then Jack caught Mamie falling off the ladder and said, "See, we're always there for each other."

Mamie said, "Yes, I will marry you. But please keep it between us until I tell Annie and Billy. Why, they'll have a manure fit!" she declared with a big grin.

She knew they would worry when they found out, and this did seem out of her character. But she thought, Here I am driving horses in a carriage while moving people from place to place doing a man's job; why worry about me? She smiled to herself, thinking, At least I know they care.

Back at the Bronsdon homestead, Billy was just getting back from the city. He had made a delivery in Roxbury and met up with a friend for lunch near their office on Merchants Row by the waterfront. The Union Oyster House was just a few steps away, and they served the best oyster chowder around.

He was meeting Alex A. Will from the Canton area not far from Readville. Alex was in the sand and stone business, using machines for screening stone while separating the sand used in making cement. He would haul wagonloads of material to be delivered to building sites. He and Billy helped each other from time to time.

Alex had a contract with a company that made his machinery for separating stones from soil. The company was well known for making equipment that was being shipped to Cuba to process sugarcane.

CHAPTER 25

# Cuba

⎯⎯⎯

BENJAMIN F. BRADFORD, A GENIUS and an inventor, was the superintendent of the American Tool and Machine Company of Hyde Park when it was formed in 1864. The company, which was being subsidized by the US government, manufactured turret and hand lathes, chucks, brass finishing tools, milling machines, and pulleys. It also designed and manufactured the sugar refining machinery used to press and extract the juice from raw canes. Bradford's patented centrifugal for purifying was in use at almost every large sugar refinery throughout the United States, the West Indies, and beyond. The machines were being sent aboard steamships out of the port of Boston, but the company was getting reports of so much damage that it was becoming a lost cause.

The principal factory was at Hyde Park. It had four brick buildings: the main machine shop, a blacksmith shop, a small machine shop, and a large foundry. The shop also contained the pattern area, drafting room, and carpenter shop. On the ground floor were the office and loading docks with railroad spurs.

Morill Smith was the broker in charge of the project. He was trying to get Alex to make the trip with his next shipment and follow the freight to see where the problem was. "In good condition" was stamped on the ship's paperwork. The damage was being done after delivery in Cuba.

Alex absolutely could not go. The thought of being on the ocean like that made him sweat profusely. "Billy," Alex said in his loud, gravelly tone, "how would you like an all-expense-paid trip?"

"To Cuba?" Billy replied.

They had lunch and joked about such an odd adventure. Besides, Billy was sure that Annie would have strong objections.

Alex told him the arrangements had been made for himself and his wife, so Annie could go on the excursion as well and have a grand time.

This hit him like a boat paddle. "She'll never go!"

Alex explained that the insurance company was demanding that a group of qualified agents go and track the shipment, or they would not insure future cargo. "You could do this. You're in the hauling trade, and that makes you a qualified agent. There is no one else I know whom I would give a recommendation to do this."

Billy, half-serious and half-joking, said, "You're serious, Alex, aren't you?" He said he needed to talk to Annie. He was intrigued himself. This was a once-in-a-lifetime opportunity. "I've never been farther than Maine. But a basic question we'll both have is when will this take place?"

Though he was fully expecting Annie to be dead set against this trip, she actually found the idea exciting. Who could ever have dreamed of something like this?

Billy smiled and told Annie he'd talk to Alex the next day for the details of when they would leave.

Annie said, "We?"

"Sure, that is what I was talking about. We can both go. It's all expenses paid."

"Get the details, and we'll talk," she said.

This was in mid-September of 1909, and it figured to be about a sixty-day round trip, which included seeing the machinery run while still on the island. The time it took to assemble the machinery they could use for relaxing. They were scheduled to depart Boston and sail to New York, where they would board the steam ship *Curitiba*.

Overall, the journey would take six weeks. They'd leave Boston on October 29, 1909; the trip from New York to Cuba would take from three to five days, depending on the weather. Now that she had the dates, Annie's answer was a firm no. "I will not be going. As it is, you will miss Thanksgiving."

Billy said, "Well, I'll be home for Christmas."

"You had better be," said Annie.

The US government had been trying to establish better relations with Cuba for years. There had been turmoil ever since President McKinley had decided to intervene in the country's politics in 1898. Now, ten years later, the United States was again trying to establish relations after intervening in a strong-armed election in 1906. Then President Roosevelt had sent Howard Taft to quell the situation. He and Assistant Secretary of State Robert Bacon were instrumental in preventing more bloodshed. This country so close to its shores had a strategic advantage for military use, and the United States wanted to keep that advantage over everyone.

The Munson Steamship Line was founded in 1899 by Walter D. Munson, who built a freight line from the United States to Cuba. His line encompassed ports in the eastern Caribbean.

Ship to the left is *Curityba*

The steamship *Curityba* departed out of Montauk on Long Island. Just as many ships have done for many years carrying material, food and people. *Curityba* would make many trips between New York and the West Indies, which included Cuba; Haiti; and the Dominican Republic, then called Hispaniola. The West Indies had been a major trading point since before 1750. Trade ships had been selling black men and women captured in Africa creating colonies of workers. The British had been using slaves as trade before 1600 and by 1850 were quite efficient at it. Cuba's sugar plantations, which had been built by slaves, now produced huge quantities of cane sugar. Harvesting was done by hand with machetes, and the cane was collected in bundles. It was then crushed to extract the juices and boiled down to sugar crystals. The machinery being sent from the factories in Hyde Park would help revolutionize the sugar industry

This was where Morill Smith got involved with the processing of cane, using roller-mill machinery to pulverize the stalks, which yielded more sugar. He was not a machinist or a manufacturer; he was a broker *the middle-man*. He had made contacts and set up offices in various areas of Cuba, as the company needed to be established within that country to be able to operate.

Smith was one of a group of Boston businessmen who built shops, warehouses, and offices for manufacturing goods for foreign trade between 1898 and 1920. Hyde Park was a major hub, with metalworks and rail access to the port of Boston. Alex Will had met Morill Smith while attending a meeting when the Boston group first became established, and it was all based on American Tool and Machine of Hyde Park. They were making machinery for companies like Sturtevant, which manufactured heating equipment. Alex had knowledge of stone-crushing plants and sluice boxes for separating stones, pea stone, sand, and even gold. He was also known for his expertise in hauling massive loads. Billy and Alex had been friends for years. Alex was a regular rider with the carriage service and had become one of Mamie's favorite fares.

The trip was organized by Morill Smith, forty-nine years old and living in Swampscott, Massachusetts. Herbert Stone, thirty-eight, from Salem, Massachusetts, was a patternmaker for American Tool and was traveling with his wife, Eva Stone, thirty-six. Leroy B. Annis, forty-eight, was a steelworker from Saint Johnsbury, Vermont. Leroy was about six feet six inches tall and had to weigh three hundred pounds, all muscle. William F. Raymond, fifty-three, and Willis Bradshaw, thirty-five, were farmers from Concord, Vermont. Then there was William C. Bronsdon, forty-one, who was in hauling and transportation.

It didn't take them very long to figure out why things were not working properly, finding that the machines were being taken apart more than intended and not reassembled properly. Then they got pulled to their destination on carts and at times on the backs of mules and men being rattled about.

The machines were a nightmare to reassemble properly. With Smith's direction, Mr. Stone drew up a sketch for a wagon to haul the machine properly. Leroy Annis, working with a local blacksmith, was able to assemble a sturdy frame. Billy was off finding wood planking for the flatbed of a wagon. Mr. Raymond and Bradshaw scouted out suitable wheels. Then, with a group of local laborers, they assembled a usable transport wagon. They loaded a machine the way it was intended and helped with the delivery.

The trip was a great success.

When the group was boarding the ship to head home, Morrill arranged for each man to receive a two-and-a-half-gallon wooden cask of some fine Cuban rum.

After its fight for independence was won on May 20, 1902, and becoming the world's top sugar producer, the Cuban nation became known for fine rum. The military personnel who had been stationed there since 1898 acquired a taste for this smooth elixir. Between 1900 and 1919, Cuban rum exports soared. In 1909 more than six million gallons were produced, with nearly two million gallons exported.

The trip back north to New York was much smoother than it had been going south; the Gulf Stream helped move the ship along nicely. Once in New York, they were put aboard the Norwegian ship *Karin* and returned to Boston on December 18, 1909.

Billy was very happy to see Boston again, and there was something he had never noticed until then: "The city has a familiar smell that, if I close my eyes, I know."

While he had been in Cuba, everyone else had needed to step up and help keep the business running. Murch took over the office and scheduling completely. Mamie started collecting the morning slips from the train station and bringing them back for Murch. They now found that Billy didn't have it as easy as they had thought. A tremendous amount of planning was required, it seemed, but it was mostly habit to Billy, and he didn't find it difficult; he had his routine. They still had to do their regular work as well, but somehow, it all got done.

Now with Billy home, Readville and the Bronsdons could get back to normal.

Again, Billy thought, My house has a familiar smell that if I close my eyes, I know where I am.

Home.

CHAPTER 26

# Mamie the Ambassador

MAMIE MADE A POINT OF having afternoon tea with Annie. She would tell her the plans she and Jack were making. She was nervous and acting strangely. Annie asked her if the monthly fairy was visiting. Mamie turned pink and laughed. "No!"

Annie laughed as well and told her she was glad she was there; she wanted to talk to her about something. She told Mamie that she was concerned about young Avis, who was now eighteen. She was seeing a boy.

"My goodness, Annie, are you sure? What would make you think such a thing? *Oh my!*" Mamie said, quite sarcastically. Then she began to laugh and said, "Annie, she is eighteen. Don't you remember this is what happens, and it's good? What do you want, an old maid?"

Annie said, "He's part Indian, and I don't like it one bit."

Mamie said, "I see."

"Could you talk to her for me, Mary, my dear sister?"

"Of course. Avis and I talk all the time." With that she left, her news untold for now.

Next afternoon, Mamie was watering Pegasus and caught sight of Avis collecting eggs in the back area of the barn. She called to her to come see her when she was finished. Soon Avis was walking over to Mamie with her apron filled with eggs.

Mamie asked if Avis could help her for a little while and then suggested she bring the eggs in and let her mother know where she was going.

137

When Avis came back, Mamie said, "Let's take a drive. I have to pick something up." With that, they climbed onto the carriage, Mamie shook the reins, and they were off.

Heading toward the parkway, she asked Avis about the young man her mother said she was seeing, which made Avis nervous. Mamie asked, "What's wrong?"

Avis didn't answer, pausing for a few minutes. Then Avis asked if Mamie disliked Indians, too.

Mamie then told her she knew about the young man she had been seeing from her mother and that he was part Indian.

Avis asked if Mamie had a problem with this, and she answered that she didn't even know who exactly they were talking about. Mamie said, "I do not prejudge anyone. Does he have both parents living with him?"

"Yes."

"Where do they live?"

"Sharon. He has started working for the railroad at the station as a freight man, and they send him to Readville at times. That was how I met him. He was in the diner buying coffee and asked if I wanted some, so we had coffee."

"Well, that was very nice of him. How old is he?"

Avis paused and then said, "Twenty-four, and he is very polite."

"Sharon, you say? Give me his name. I have a good friend in Sharon. I'll ask of his reputation."

Avis said "Ernest, but he said to call him Ernie. His full name is Ernie Rau."

Mamie was flabbergasted and in an astonished voice said, "The German boy?"

"Yes, why? Is it bad to be a German, too?"

"No, no, no. I know him and his whole family. I am friends with his mother, which is where the Indian comes in. His mother's name is Edith," Mamie said. "She is a baker at the Blue Bird Café in Canton. I've known her quite some time. I also know Ernie. He is a very nice young man—strong and fit as a fiddle. I'm up there two or three times a week. His father is very nice as well."

Avis gave her a big smile, and Mamie dropped a tear or two and then said to Avis, "Can you keep a secret?"

"Yes, Aunt Mamie," she replied.

"Well, Jack McDonough has asked me to marry him, and he's going to build us a grand new house."

Avis had a look of bewilderment, as she couldn't picture Mamie and a man anyway, but married?

Mamie said, "What? I thought you may be too young and now I'm too old?"

They both laughed, and Mamie told her she could come to her wedding and then said not to say anything to her mother. Mamie planned to speak to Annie that night and would give her endorsement of Ernie.

When she finished for the day, Mamie stopped at the house to see Annie and told her all about the Rau family of Germans who lived in Sharon. Then she told her that she knew Ernie. Mamie said, "Now that I know who we are discussing—and what a nice young man, too."

Annie didn't get excited but needed to digest this news and thanked her sister for her help.

Then Mamie said, "Oh, look at the time. Got to go. Jack is coming for supper." As she opened the door to leave, she blurted out, "Oh, and we're getting married!"

Annie screamed, "*What?*"

Mamie walked quickly away with Annie yelling, "Come back here!"

Without turning around, she hollered back, "You have a lot to digest. I'll see you tomorrow," and she was off.

# CHAPTER 27

# Buildings and Relationships

MAMIE WAS A LITTLE LATE getting home and hadn't even started supper when Jack arrived. She apologized for not having supper started. "Not a problem," he replied.

She suggested making up sandwiches, and then they could just sit on Jack's porch and enjoy the evening with Blue Hill and the meadow as a bonus. He thought that was a fine idea, and she got some things together. It was a beautiful evening, and there was a faint smell of ocean air, which was not very far away, actually.

She was up early next day for a fare in Milton. Freddy was already in the barn getting her horse harnessed, while she checked all the wheel hubs for grease and made sure that the rein connections were tight.

When she turned to say something to Freddy, she was startled by Annie, arms crossed and with a stern face. "You were saying, young lady?"

Mamie reacted by saying, "Good morning!"

"You know what I mean, Mary. You're getting married? To Jack? He drinks like the devil, and he's friends with Tut Coughlin to boot."

Mamie replied, "So he likes to nip a little. Lots of men do. And he supports himself just fine, owns quite a bit of land around here, and his gardening skill is second to none."

"Where will you live?" Annie asked.

Mamie explained the new house Jack had already started and that it was going to be beautiful. "Jack is very different to me than he seems to most. I do love his company," she said.

Annie had breakfast on the table for Billy and Freddy after the early chores, and while pouring coffee for Billy, she told him about Mamie marrying Jack. He never even flinched while reading the day's schedule. Then turned and told Annie that he liked Jack very much and that he already knew, as Jack had come to talk to him, knowing he watched out for Mary.

"I just wanted her to tell you. Didn't want it coming from me first. That might have caused a problem."

Freddy ate and listened and was confident in feeling that Billy always seemed to know what to do. For that matter, he always seemed to know everything that was going on. That was Billy for sure: quiet and confident, and when he spoke, it was with authority.

"Now if it were me, Annie, I would tell her that if there was anything you could help with, please let you know."

Annie said no more at this time, and they finished breakfast in peace.

Many Readville residents were wondering what Jack was up to with all the loads he was going by with. They were used to seeing him hauling wood, but he normally brought it somewhere to do a job for someone. Now he was bringing all this material down to his own property.

Late one morning, actually closer to noontime, Jack stopped by the Bronsdon livery stable to see Billy. Freddy was coming out of the barn and stopped to see if Jack needed help with anything. Jack said he was looking for William, and Freddy smiled and told him that he'd be right out; he just went to get something in the house.

Freddy loved horses and asked about Jack's horse, "What's this guy's name?"

"Clyde," Jack replied.

"Might I water him, Mr. McDonough?"

"Sure can, my boy. Thank you."

Billy walked over to Jack, reaching out to shake his hand, and said, "Well, what might my future brother-in-law be up to?"

Jack smiled lightly and said, "Well, William, I'm building this new house, and my wagon and horse can handle the lumber pretty well, but I need to get some big granite blocks down here from Roslindale. You have equipment to move them. I would like to hire you. The rock is coming out of the quarry in Quincy, but I made a deal with Canniff, the monument company. They have a pulley rig set up to load, and I'll rig something up at my place for unloading."

Billy said he'd be happy to help out and that he had a rig with a lifting device. "What kind of weight are we talking?" he asked.

"Substantial," Jack replied. "They'll be eight feet long, but the widths will vary. Nothing more than three feet, though, and all a foot thick." Billy was surprised by the "eight feet," and Jack said, "The basement will be eight feet high."

Billy scrunched one eye and said to Jack, "Let's take a ride after lunch."

"OK." Jack was about to leave, when Billy stopped him and said, "Come on in and have some lunch with us, brother. Annie will be delighted."

Freddy had all he could do not to laugh out loud.

"Why, thank you, William. I'll take you up on that." And Jack went into the house with them.

Annie had the table set, and when she looked and saw Jack, she looked again as if her eyes were playing a trick. "Well, if it isn't Jack McDonough," she said.

Billy spoke up and asked that she set another place for Jack. "He'll be joining us."

"Well, sit down, you three. There's cold shoulder," she said, half-joking and with a bit sarcasm, "and potato salad with hard-cooked egg."

"Jack, try one of Annie's pickled green tomatoes and some of that horseradish she and Mamie made. It'll curl your eyebrows."

After lunch Billy asked Jack, "When we go over to Roslindale, can we get a piece to bring back?"

"We can get whatever you want to bring back. My lot of stone is all there, and I'm ready back at my place. I have the brothers who do the grave digging over at Fairview Cemetery doing my foundation hole, and they're just about done."

"We'll take my heavy rig," Billy said, and he told Freddy to get it ready with two of his Percheron draft horses.

Billy had acquired these horses, actually four of them, from the government when they closed down a base in Boston. That was also where he got the wagon with the hoist; it had been used to move the massive cannons during the war. This breed of horse actually came from France. It is a mix of Arabian and Clydesdale. Billy figured two should be sufficient. He told Freddy to come along. "You may learn something."

The freight run itself was pretty straightforward except the last half-mile. It was up a hill, whether they came in from the Hyde Park side or through Milton. So it was off through Hyde Park and a straight run up the avenue toward Jamaica Plain.

Billy directed his team to where he needed them, and backed them up to put the wagon gantry to lower the stones in place. He attached a chain around one stone and then told Freddy to start pulling the gantry chains that would lift it up.

Billy asked if Freddy felt strong today, and as he asked, the stone moved and then lifted off the wagon deck. Freddy blurted out how easily the stone moved. Then Billy told him to pick up the pole next to him and push against the huge rock. When he did this, the rock easily moved along the gantry rail and hovered over the foundation hole.

The cemetery men were there to put them in place, as they said, "just like dropping in a headstone," while Jack made sure they were plumb. Start off straight and plumb, the only way to work.

Freddy just kept talking about how amazing it was to move such heavy stones so easily.

Billy told him, "Just remember, never get any part of you under what you are lifting. If that rock slipped its chain, it'd likely go right through the bottom of the wagon and you, too, if you're not careful. Always think first, son. Tell me, Freddy, what do you think of Jack?"

"I like him, but he has terrible breath, and Aunt Annie doesn't like him. But he knows how to get things done, like building."

"That's right, kid. He has skill to learn from, and you saw what we did today. Jack knew I could get that done—that's why he came to me. And you are right, he knows how to get things done. And Jack had lunch with Annie today. Need I say more?"

CHAPTER 28

# Good Time Ahead

MAMIE'S LIFE WAS GOOD. SHE had the carriage service, driving patrons who to her were friends. They would always ask her to come on trips with them and travel the world, all expenses paid. She always declined those trips; she felt too much responsibility at home.

There were times when she felt bad for some of these friends, knowing that they needed to travel to get away from this part of life. Mamie didn't have that situation. She enjoyed every day, driving through Readville to Milton especially; it was peaceful.

Now she was going to marry Jack and live in the new wonderful house he was building just for her. She would have the use of gardens and a beautiful, big kitchen with a hand pump and some of the best water anyone could have in this area—pure, with no factories, houses, or people for that matter. Jack always knew he was getting water from the edge of Fowl Meadow. The water was crystal clear and very cold year round, with very little iron, so it was good, sweet water.

"How could I not love this place? It's Eden. Look up there!"

Mamie loved Blue Hill. It was her place to be, and she loved the experience itself. Not just driving her horse but the sights and smells of the forest in fall, or spring coming on, with the peepers screaming in the meadow.

"God, this is lovely. I must be the luckiest woman on earth."

The wealthy from Boston regularly made trips to Cape Cod. This meant leaving very early in the morning, hoping to make it to Bourne by nightfall, where friends would put them up in grand fashion. They'd continue on the next day, arriving in Wellfleet by dusk. It was about 110 miles from Boston, but the roads were rutted, and it was very slow going.

Some of the wealthier families owned ships and would sail out of Boston Harbor and across Plymouth Bay. With the right wind, the thirty-two-mile trip would take most of one day.

This particular Friday afternoon, Mamie got finished early and left without saying much. She headed home and got cleaned up. She soon met up with Jack, and they headed off in his wagon, driving to the Canton Depot. Then they took the 3:00 p.m. train to Boston, telling no one, and walked over to city hall and bought their marriage license.

Jack had his lawyer friend Harry Dean from Readville, who was also a justice of the peace, meeting them. Harry lived just up on Chester Street near Milton Street. His house, built by Jack McDonough, was a three-decker.

Harry had arranged to marry them in a civil ceremony. Mamie's friend Kerry Kelly was with the Eustis family in their main home downtown and came to stand up for her.

The three of them and the judge went to Durgin Park for a most festive dinner, featuring massive ribs of beef, pots of beans, and delicious popovers with au jus. Harry bought dinner for all, and the judge arranged a room—his personal room—at the Parker House Hotel for them for the night.

Next morning, Mamie was up early and ready to go to church. This would be a very special service. She wanted to attend at the cathedral where the bishop of Boston said Mass, and Sunday was always a High Mass.

Jack wanted coffee, and that would come to be a special treat. The Parker House had a restaurant known to be in a class with those in New York and Paris. Jack sat at a table and was served the best cup of coffee he had ever had pass his lips.

When Mamie sat down, Jack said, "Oh, the coffee, my dear. Oh, the coffee!" Mamie took a sip and said, "Oh, Jack. Oh, the coffee," and smiled.

The waiter then put out a plate with some rolls and butter and a bit of jam. Mamie took a roll that was as soft as a fresh marshmallow, put a little butter on it, and tasted it, exclaiming, "Oh, Jack, the rolls are amazing as well. I can't tell if everything is better because I'm so happy that we married!"

They would later find out from Harry Dean that those were the world-renowned Parker House rolls.

Mamie did go to the cathedral, and the bishop did say Mass, and Mary Catherine McDonough did get Jack to tag along, saying, "Only for you, my dear Mamie."

They had lunch at the Union Oyster House, a big plate of oysters on the half shell and bowls of seafood chowder.

Then it was a short walk over to South Station to get the train back to Canton. Jack had put Clyde, his horse, up to board with a friend of Mamie's at the depot.

They got back into Readville just in time for Sunday dinner at Annie's house. When they pulled in, Billy was just closing the barn doors. He walked over, saying how surprised he had been not to see Mamie that morning. He knew that she had a fare who always went to early church services. "But of course you would make sure they got taken care of. Freddy told me you arranged for him to help out."

"Just needed to go out for a bit, Billy."

"Not a problem, Mary. I'm happy to see it. Come in for dinner."

Annie had a nice pork loin roasted with carrot, potato, parsnips, and onions, and her gravy was amazing, with a texture like silk. As they finished, Mamie got up to pour coffee for everyone. Standing between Billy and Annie, she started talking aloud about her last day or so and the events that had occurred, and while painting her tale like a picture, she suddenly came out with, "And then we got our marriage license and got married!"

Just then Annie coughed and choked on her coffee for a bit. "Mary, you did?"

"Yes. We had a wonderful time and spent the past day and night downtown, eating some of the best food, umm, outside of your kitchen." Mamie laughed out loud.

Billy got up and walked into his parlor to a cabinet in the corner and took out a bottle and two snifters. Coming back to the dining table, he suggested that he and Jack have a drink of rum. "It's from the cask they gave each of us in the West Indies. It's made in Cuba and very good," he said, as he made two heavy pours and raised his glass.

"A toast to Mary and Jack. May you have a long and happy marriage."

Billy and Jack toasted with their rum and Annie and Mamie with their coffee.

Freddy had milk.

# CHAPTER 29

# Guess Who's Coming to Dinner

JACK WAS JUST ABOUT TO the point at which he could tell Mamie that the house was done. She asked what he thought of inviting Annie and Billy for Easter dinner. Hoping she would ask that, he said it would be fine by him.

Mamie was enthralled. "What will I cook?"

Jack suggested, "Leg of lamb, my dear?"

"Yes, Jack, a leg of lamb from Butler's farm. Kerry is friends with them, and I can do this."

Jack said, "I know," with a smile.

Mamie's new kitchen was bigger than most. Jack wanted her to be happy, and this was wonderful to Mamie. At times she would stand at her window over the kitchen sink looking at her hill, as she called it, not wanting to be anywhere else.

Mamie was home.

Jack owned much of the area on this side of Fowl Meadow. The land had been part of the training camp during the war. When it was closed down in the late 1800s, Jack's father had been paid in options on the land. When Hyde Park grew into a bustling village, he started buying the options for pennies on the dollar. The government wanted the property off its books, and he bought whatever he could. This would pay off nicely in the future.

Jack had lots in other areas of Readville as well, always close to the railroad for his lumber business.

There was an area just over the railroad bridge that Jack named McDonough Court and built houses to sell. He always had something going on for profit.

Henry was…we'll say "different." No, he was odd. Actually, Henry was as batty as a belfry, likely autistic. He was younger than Jack, who had set him up in a home on the avenue to Hyde Park. Jack paid monthly for his room and board to make sure he had a place to eat and sleep.

Henry tried to work, but his mind would not focus for longer than a few minutes, and then he would just wander off and find something to write on. Almost anything was good enough for him to write on, and he would often copy something else that was nearby, signs or news articles, but what Henry enjoyed most was poetry. He would thumb through newspapers looking for poems and, in very nice handwriting, copy them into one of his journals.

Now that Mamie was part of Jack's life, she suggested that Henry come to dinner, at least on special occasions and holidays. Jack was very happy to hear this and would dutifully pick him up whenever Mamie wanted him there.

Mamie had a beautiful kitchen and bountiful garden at her disposal. She canned regularly, filling the cellar with jars of tomatoes, jams, jelly, pickles, green beans…things that would not keep through the winter otherwise. The root cellar would hold carrots, parsnips, winter squash, turnip, and pumpkins.

She found that, with patience, she could show Henry how to help her with canning and actually almost anything that was repetitive. Henry enjoyed doing the same thing over and over, so this was good for him, and Mamie liked the help and company.

They could go into the garden, pick a whole row of beans, and have them prepared and jarred by lunch. Henry loved her bean salad, and Mamie knew that, but she always waited for him to ask for it because he got excited and happy knowing she was making it just for him.

She enjoyed Henry's company, and it was good for him to get out. They both loved the ocean, which was only seven miles east of Readville, just the other side of Blue Hill. Mamie was quite familiar with the route to Quincy Bay and Wollaston, which was more than two miles of sandy beach. She and Henry would go to dig clams there at low tide. The tide tables were listed in Jack's *Old Farmer's Almanac*, and Mamie wanted to be at the water one hour before low tide.

Digging clams was another repetitious activity that Henry was very good at. The mud really smelled at low tide, but it was loaded with soft-shell steamer clams, and using some of Jack's gardening tools, they could easily dig a bushel basket full in a very short period of time.

The hardest part was getting Henry to stop digging. Mamie would tell him that if he kept digging, there would be no clams left for next time. That always worked.

Heading back to Readville with the clams covered in wet burlap to keep them fresh, they would stop at Florence Murdock's to give her and Tom some bounty and then on to give Annie some, too. Then it was home to have hot steamers with melted butter. Henry loved them, but he only ate the neck part, which was fine by Mamie and Jack. They both loved the bellies, the bigger the better.

There were always leftover clams, and Mamie would clean them all to make clam chowder the next day. She started with small cubes of salt pork, or fatback as it was called, which got rendered down. Next, she added onion and celery, when it was available. Then she added some flour to make a roux, then water and potato cubes, and let that simmer and meld. Then the saved clams and a cup of heavy cream went in. Just before serving the chowder, Mamie would add a piece of butter to make it silky and rich. They ate it with soda crackers. Jack liked the crackers crumbled into his chowder, and Henry did the same, as he assumed he should.

When Mamie had some leftover chowder, she had another use for it. Her friend Edith Getchell, Ernie Rau's mother, had taught her to use the chowder for pie. She would add some crushed crackers as a thickener and pour it into a pie crust. Mamie's clam pie was a favorite of Henry's. Billy enjoyed that combination of clam and crust made with lard, a perfect match. He loved it with lots of black pepper.

April 7 was a chilly Easter Sunday. Jack had some of the garden started—peas were in, and lettuce was coming up. Crocuses were done and daffodils blooming. The land was coming back from a long, cold winter.

Jack told Mamie that his almanac said the weather should brighten, and it would be a nice warm day. She had been up since 3:00 a.m. getting her dinner preparations in order. There would be ten for dinner.

Jack set up a long table with some planks and actually came up with ten good chairs. There was a big leg of lamb, and Mamie had all the side dishes. Annie was bringing a surprise dessert.

Billy had his chores to do, and Freddy helped out by taking Mamie's patrons to church. They called it a day early, and everyone was at the McDonoughs' by early afternoon. Jack brought Billy out to show off his garden up close. This was very impressive, and Billy could see the passion Jack had for his land. He also got to see what his loads of manure went into.

Looking out across the meadow and up at Blue Hill, he said to Jack, "She's right."

Dinner was a huge success, and Mamie looked forward to doing this again. Then Annie asked, "Who wants dessert?"

When she went to the kitchen counter for it, Mamie began to get up to help, but Annie told her to sit; it was her turn.

When she came to the table, she had a big, white-frosted cake and a candle burning on it. Now Billy spoke up and with a toast congratulated Mamie and Jack, first saying congratulations to Mr. and Mrs. John McDonough on the marriage, and then to Jack for building this wonderful house, and another to toast Mamie's first dinner party, which was a great success.

Billy and Jack went out with a couple of very good cigars that William had acquired.

# CHAPTER 30

# For Better or Worse

THE TIMES WERE CHANGING, AND automobiles were becoming more and more common, Mamie still drove her carriage, but her rigorous schedule was in decline.

Having a barn to use at their new home, Billy let her keep the carriage there, and she rotated horses, keeping one at the Bronsdon stable. She loved driving with her horses and was actually beginning to enjoy her newfound freedom, still driving some of her patrons but not having a full schedule. Now she had time for herself, caring for the house, and visiting friends.

When she paid visits to Edith at the Blue Bird in Canton, Ernie would sometimes hitch a ride back to Readville with her to visit Avis. He was working for the railroad, so he could ride the train back to the Sharon Depot going home.

He was a strong young man, and his mother, Edith, noticed that he was cooking when she was out and doing pretty well at it. She had him start coming to the Blue Bird, so she could teach him some of her skills. He was a natural and was soon helping in the kitchen with the head cook while learning from his mother the art of pie crust. He was not only good at cooking, he also enjoyed spending time with her.

He started showing his younger brother, Herbie, what to do, and soon he was cooking as well. Edith was very happy knowing they could cook for themselves, which was very important in her mind.

Ernie seemed to take to almost anything he set out to do. He could grow a garden, care for animals, drive a horse and carriage, and cook, and he was strong as an ox.

He had grown into a man.

This one particular day, Ernie was riding back with Mamie, and with her being so easy to talk to, he told her that he was going to ask Avis to marry him. Without even a pause, she gave him a quick hug and said, "It's a wonderful idea. When will you ask her?"

Now that he'd actually said it out loud to someone, his palms were sweaty, and he got nervous. "What will her parents say?" he asked.

Mamie said, "You go take care of asking her father. I'll help with Annie. Mr. Bronsdon should be fine."

Once the moment was right, Ernie popped the question.

Avis cautiously said yes, and then Ernie told her that he had confided in Mamie, and she was willing to help with her mother. "I'll talk to your father on my own," he said.

At first, she was surprised that he had talked to Mamie, and then she was relieved that he had.

The following Saturday, Avis invited Ernie to supper and hoped Mamie might be there, too. Ernie took an early train to Readville, as he wanted to talk to Mr. Bronsdon first, and by chance he found him at the depot getting his schedule straight. Billy saw him coming and reached out to shake his hand as he approached. Ernie had a very strong grip, and Billy took note.

Ernie asked to talk a bit, and they took a bench at the depot. Getting right to the point, he asked Mr. Bronsdon if he would approve of his asking Avis to wed.

After a short pause and a bit of dissertation, Ernie began to feel sick, not actually hearing any of Billy's words until he said, "I think you'll make a fine son-in-law, Ernest," with another strong handshake. Then Billy said, "Now for your future mother-in-law," and smiled.

After a fine meatloaf dinner, Avis began clearing the table, and Billy stopped everyone and asked them to have a seat. Everyone was still sitting, and Mamie happened to stop in for coffee just then.

Billy was saying that there was some news they all should hear together. "You too, Mamie. Have a seat." He turned to Ernie, saying, "Go on, son. Give us the good news."

Ernie spoke up, half-asking and half-explaining. It was actually news only to Annie, but she had seen this day coming and was somewhat prepared. That sort of startled Billy, as it did not sound like the Annie he was used to, and the preparations began.

Edith could not have been happier. Though she did not know Avis very well, she did know how polite Avis was and that she came from good roots and a strong family.

After Avis and Ernie's wedding, Billy set them up with his house at 19 Hamilton Street to live in until they were well on their feet. They were very happy there in Readville.

Ernie soon turned the area behind the barn into a big garden and showed Billy he was a capable gardener. The horse manure made everything grow nicely, and Ernie had little planting methods picked up from his mother.

When Ernie was young he spent short periods in Acushnet learning the "Indian ways," he would spend two or three weeks each summer camping with his mother's people. All his brothers were expected to do this, and though most didn't care for it, Ernie actually enjoyed it. Acushnet was where he learned to dress out rabbits, deer, and birds for food. They ate oysters raw, fresh from the ocean, and steamer clams cooked on fires covered in seaweed. The taste was incredible, with the smoke and seaweed flavoring the food.

Spring would bring mackerel to the bay, and the water was thick with fish. The men would set out nets and draw in huge numbers of fish that would be set up on racks to dry for later use.

They ate cod, haddock, flounder, and striped bass in the summer, along with clams and crabs. Lobster was plentiful, but they knew the best time to eat it was after September, when the shells would be hard and full of sweet meat.

Deer was harvested in cold weather to avoid summer worms. Rabbit was always fair game, and his relatives taught him to field dress a rabbit in less than a minute.

This was part of his life, and he loved it, but away from there, he did not tell anyone about being part Indian. It was a time when they were not considered part of the white man's culture, even though they had been here long before the white people. There were always the bad apples in the bunch, like Injun Joe who lived in a wooded area near Sprague Pond. He was always getting drunk and being thrown in jail for rowdiness, but Indians were not supposed to drink, and that alone could get them arrested. It was usually a cop's decision. ("Constable on patrol" was where the term *cop* originated, though not necessarily in Readville.)

Ernie was light skinned with German features, blue eyes, and a German last name, so he fit right in everywhere. The Indian Wars, like General Custer's bloody massacre out West, were still fresh in many people's minds.

Still working on the railroad, Billy was able to help get Ernie reassigned to the Readville Depot. He was still cooking part time at the Blue Bird as well.

Mamie was at the Bronsdon stable daily and watching how nicely his garden was doing, telling Jack about it. Ernie was finding wild lilies and transplanting them all around the garden. Mamie suggested that Ernie go down and see Jack; he had many perennials that she was sure he'd share.

Mamie was getting gardening jobs for Ernie with some of her friends in Milton. Some wanted ornamental flower areas, while others wanted herb and kitchen gardens. He was busy seven days a week, but he was making money. She had been suggesting this opportunity to Jack, but that was not his cup of tea. He had his gardens and would be digging for himself; that was enough for him.

Early one morning in April, Billy heard some noise behind the barn, and when he walked around back, there was Ernie moving a pile of manure while making another. Billy scratched his head, thought a second, and asked, "Why on earth are you moving that pile?"

Ernie looked up, sweating to beat the band, and then he reached down and picked up a massive night crawler and handed it to his father-in-law. Still without a word, he dug the shovel in and lifted up a pile of almost coal-black soil. Ernie said to Billy, "The manure feeds the worms, and we fish with the worms. The bigger ones stay under the pile, and the small, wiggly ones break down the pile."

Billy was impressed and said, "Well, let's go fishing!"

Ernie told Billy why he was actually digging to the bottom for the soil, coal black and rich, loaded with worms. Ernie said he had a job to plant a garden area up in Milton, and he wanted to use this for his planting. He knew from past experience how well it worked. He loaded up some soil, and the men went fishing.

They were going right past Green Street in Milton and could drop the soil off for Ernie to use later. He knew how lush the plants would grow in this fortified mixture.

Fishing was a favorite activity of Ernie's, and he was off any chance he had. There were kettle ponds scattered about the Blue Hill area. One in particular, Houghton's Pond, situated in Milton right next to the foot of Blue Hill, was spring fed, clear, and cold, with a variety of fish and deep enough to hold trout. They need cold, deep water to survive hot summers.

Billy liked to fish as well and frequently tagged along with his son-in-law. Ernie told Billy about his mother teaching him that their people, the Wampanoag Indians, had called this pond Hoosic-Whisick long before it was Houghton Pond. The area was part of nearby Braintree until 1754, when Ebenezer Houghton bought 340 acres to farm, and his pond became Houghton's Pond.

Billy and Ernie were heading there to fish one Sunday afternoon when Ernie suggested going to a favorite pond of his in Sharon. Close to his mother's house on Pond Street, there was a sawmill, and it was powered by a waterfall on the pond. That was what it was called, too—Sawmill Pond. He told Billy there were trout as long as your arm.

Billy smiled, smirked, and said, "Show me these monsters."

The pond wasn't very big, less than half the size of Houghton's, and fed from a stream at one end that was joined somewhere to the Neponset River area.

Before Billy tossed a line, Ernie asked him to wait a minute, and he fumbled with the leaves on the ground, coming up with a salamander. He gave it to Billy and suggested he try it for bait. Billy hooked it through the mouth and tossed it into the pond about ten feet out.

Within seconds his pole was bent in half. While reeling it in, he joked, "My son-in-law, the outdoorsman," and pulled in an eighteen-inch brown trout.

The men had a great day fishing and stopped at Edith's to share some bounty. They had a great feed that night with fish breaded in corn meal and fried in butter.

Avis was less than thrilled. She hated trout; it was white ocean fish only for her. The smell of the fish was actually making her nauseous, and she went to lie down after supper. Annie took note and went about her cleanup. Ernie did the dishes. He was growing on Annie, for the good.

They ate together often, as Avis did not have her mother's cooking skill. Ernie would cook at home, but most days he was so busy, it was just easier to eat with their in-laws. Annie was a fine cook, and dinner was always ready about five o'clock, give or take fifteen minutes.

# CHAPTER 31

# Mamie's Red Sox

MAMIE WAS THIRTY-FOUR YEARS OLD when the newly built Fenway Park was opened. She looked forward to seeing the new palace.

Her good friend Tom Nolan had acquired tickets from a Harvard classmate for opening day and asked Mamie to join him and two friends. The date was set for April 18, 1912. Mamie had been reminding Billy she would be gone for the afternoon that day.

The weather didn't cooperate, and it rained for four days that week, Tuesday through Friday. Opening day had been scheduled for Thursday. The game was changed to Saturday, April 20, 1912, at two o'clock, and Mamie could not go to the game that day. Even though she might have been able to cancel an appointment, that was not her way; she kept her commitments.

Thomas had told Mamie he would get her to the next game he could get tickets for, and that turned out to be on Friday, April 26, 1912. The Red Sox won that game, and by chance Mamie got to see Hugh Bradley hit the first home run over the left field wall we now call the Green Monster.

The Sox had a standout season in 1912 and won the American League title with 105 wins and only 47 loses. They then beat the New York Giants to clinch the World Series.

Two years later, the Red Sox signed a new player by the name of George Herman Ruth. He had been signed to a minor-league contract with the Baltimore Orioles out of a reform school in that city. Soon after, he was traded to Boston. The nickname "Babe" was common among men who played ball, and it stuck to George, who would become Babe Ruth and give baseball a new hero of the day.

Mamie went to games whenever possible. The crowds were almost all men in fedoras smoking cigars. But Mamie was strong in her own right, and they didn't bother her.

Because of the connections the Bronsdon's had in Boston, Mamie could safely stable her rig while at the game. Billy made sure the stableman understood and took good care of Mamie so she didn't have any problem.

The Braves used Fenway Park as their home field for a few games toward the end of their memorable 1914 season. What should have been a great team right from the start turned dismal, with four wins and eighteen losses. By July they were in last place, and they lost both games of a Fourth of July doubleheader. It seemed hopeless.

Still in last place on July 18, they had a day off.

Coming back was daunting, but they began winning, moving up to fourth place. By mid-August, they were in second place. Rolling through September with twenty-five wins and six losses, they clinched the pennant and then swept the Philadelphia Athletics to win the World Series.

Fenway was new and larger than the Braves home field, the South End Grounds. Late in the season, with the amazing run the team had, many games were rescheduled to be played at Fenway to accommodate larger crowds.

Braves owner James Gaffney had dropped his plans for a new ballpark during the disastrous period that year. After such a tremendous comeback, he built a new ballpark, calling it Braves Field. It opened in August of 1915 and was the largest baseball park at the time, seating forty thousand. It was designed so spectators could be dropped off inside the park. Mamie loved driving through when she had the chance.

The Red Sox used Braves Field for home games in 1915 for larger attendance as well.

Mamie saw many games over the years; they're just too numerous to record. She always followed her favorite players. Murch would have the daily newspaper, and the scores would be right on the back page.

In 1916, since Mamie was a licensed hackney driver, she was able to drive one of her Milton patrons to the ballpark and see some games. Before the licensing requirement, anyone could work as a driver. With the licensing, drivers had to display a badge, or their carriages would be turned away.

The 1916 season was special in many ways to Mamie, the Red Sox, and the city of Boston. The team had a young pitcher, and he was having an amazing season, going twenty-three and twelve and leading the league with an ERA of 1.75.

Whether it was luck or chance, Augustus Hemenway, a wealthy philanthropist from Milton, was a regular patron of Mamie's. Actually, she drove his entire family regularly. Mr. Hemenway wanted to see Babe Ruth pitch every game he could make with his busy schedule. Knowing from his daughter that Mamie was a great fan of the Red Sox, he insisted on her driving him to games.

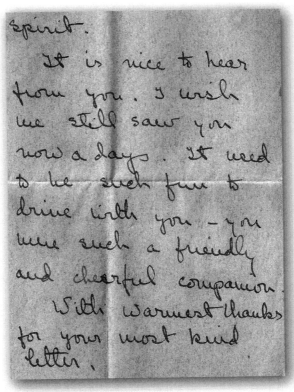

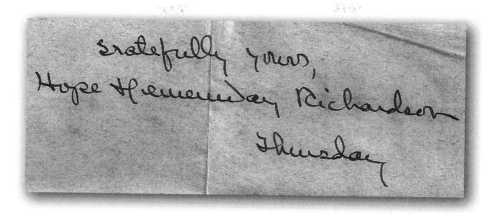

I don't think it was luck or chance; it was Mamie being herself with people, and they liked that about her. She could talk about subjects that most of her peers, being men, rough men, wouldn't admit to understanding even if they could—and forget about them singing. Being well read and attentive she could converse on many subjects and be friendly with most.

The Red Sox made it to the World Series in 1916, playing against the Brooklyn Robins, later called the Dodgers. Eddie Shore pitched the opener, which was played at Braves Field to accommodate the crowd. Game one came down to the ninth inning with the Red Sox down five to two. They then got four runs to win the opener, with Shore pitching the complete game.

Ruth was scheduled to pitch the next day, and Mamie got word that Mr. Hemenway wanted her services. She was thrilled. A World Series game! Babe Ruth was scheduled to pitch, and she would be there!

Game two was a real pitching duel between Ruth and Sherry Smith, another lefty like the Babe. They both pitched into the thirteenth inning, giving up but six hits and only one run each. The Sox would come up with four runs and win game two in the fourteenth on base hits and good managing.

The next three games were played at the newly opened Ebbet's Field in New York. The Robins took game three, but the Red Sox won games four and five for the Series win.

First thing the morning after the game, Mamie was looking for the newspaper. Murch didn't have his, telling Mamie it was late.

She left for the train depot knowing that the telegraph office would have the news she wanted. Though she realized it was Friday the thirteenth, Mamie had to know.

When she pulled up to the station, it was already clear that the Sox had won. Between 1914 and 1918, Babe Ruth was mainly considered a pitcher, and he was amazing. As he got more comfortable playing in front of big crowds, he started showing off his real talent: hitting long and frequent home runs, even during a time called the dead-ball era.

Once Ruth began showing his other talents, the Red Sox began using him in the outfield with great success. And with success came excess, nightlife, alcohol, food, and women. He enjoyed it all.

Then in 1919 this new sporting venture sent him to New York and a very turbulent history. Right after the 1919 season, Ruth was traded to the New York Yankees for cash. That same season, Ruth had broken the single-season record for home runs. From 1920 on, there would be no pennants for the Red Sox until they won the American League in 1946 and then lost the World Series to the Saint Louis Cardinals in seven games.

The grumbling began again after the largest attendance ever in Boston with close to one and a half million coming out to the park.

On that dark December day in 1919, it began to circulate that this was the Curse of the Bambino. It wouldn't be until well after Mamie died that the Sox would win a World Series again, in 2004.

Mamie did see them win, I am sure.

In 1924, the Boston Red Sox played seventy-seven games at Fenway Park, with an average attendance of 5,700 fans. These were games that took all day at times, and there were many doubleheaders. It was common for a pitcher to throw both games and bat as well. With a dreadful season of sixty-seven wins and eighty-seven losses, they came in seventh place, one up from the last-place Chicago White Sox.

This was also the Bruins first season as a new expansion team, playing at Boston Arena. They had a worse season than the Red Sox. The Bruins came in last with six wins and twenty-four losses, scoring just 49 goals and giving up 119.

Mamie went to one of the last games of that 1924 season. The Red Sox were playing the Yankees, and Babe Ruth was playing left field for New York. Many considered Ruth a traitor, but in 1924 he had forty-four home runs, and Mamie got to see him hit one that day. She would later say he actually reached up and swung the bat almost like a tomahawk, swatting the ball into the right-field seats.

His nicknames were many, including the Babe, the Great Bambino, and the Sultan of Swat. He was actually George Herman Ruth born on February 6, 1895 in Baltimore, Maryland. He played twenty-two seasons from 1914 through 1935. Ruth died in Manhattan, New York, on August 16, 1948, at the age of fifty-three.

His story is legendary.

# CHAPTER 32

# Finding His Place

ERNIE HAD A GOOD APTITUDE for working with his hands and understanding things with a practical sense, so he was a natural fit when he heard about a new factory to be opened in Cambridge, Massachusetts.

The year was 1912, and the new place was being built by Henry Ford, the automobile builder. This would be one of several plants Ford would construct to begin building his automobiles for local sales. The locations had to be on or very close to water transportation for his parts deliveries. This was another concept thought out and designed by Ford.

The building was constructed so that vehicle assembly began on the top floor. There was a track that snaked down five floors of conveyor assembly. Men worked in a coordinated assembly process from the wheels to the roof. The automobile shells gradually moved forward and down. Once a car was at ground level, it would be ready to sell.

Ernie stayed with Ford after they closed the Cambridge plant and built a new plant in Somerville in what is called Assembly Square today. It's close to the Mystic River and rail lines. In 1926, with a brand-new facility, Ernie was in on the ground floor of a great opportunity. He eventually worked his way into middle management.

Ernie was doing well by the spring of 1929, and the Ford Motor Company had 128,000 in its employ. Later in 1929, there would be a major stock market crash, and the country would fall into a depression. By August of 1931, Ford would employ only 37,000.

Avis Rau (Nana), my uncle Ernie, and Ernest P. Rau (Pa)

Ernie kept his job through the bad times because, as Henry Ford stated at that time, "The average man won't really do a day's work unless he is caught and cannot get out of it. There is plenty of work to do if people would do it."

# CHAPTER 33

# Mamie Knows Everyone

HISTORICALLY, MILTON HAS ALWAYS BEEN a wealthy town, and it attracted many people trying to live an elegant life in a quiet and comfortable setting, while still being close to an economic center. Boston and Quincy lay to its east on the Atlantic coast, at the edge of a tidal river. Milton and Blue Hills, with its surrounding woods and ponds, were quiet and without factories, saving the area from smoke, smell, and pollution. There were no trains and very few houses.

The Eustis estate was a good example of how society lived. This estate was actually a summer house at 1426 Canton Avenue, set on eighty beautiful acres. The main house was twenty-one thousand square feet, very much the grand scale of a wealthy family. William Ellery Channing Eustis hired William Ralph Emerson, cousin of Ralph Waldo Emerson, to design the house, and it was built in 1878. The gatekeeper's house, potting shed, and greenhouse were built in 1892 bordering Canton Avenue.

Once through the gate, there was a long, tree-lined driveway with huge, landscaped fields leading to the stately front entry. Mamie loved coming here, and as she drove through the property, she remembered Billy Bronsdon telling her about this land belonging to his grandfather Phinehas back in the early 1800s.

John Bronsdon, older brother of Phinehas, had lived here in the late 1700s, when it was known as the old Bronsdon place. Built in 1730, the old house saw a century of Bronsdon births and deaths before it was torn down around 1830, when John built the new house. Known to be a gentleman, John

Bronsdon was killed instantly in a tragic logging accident in the Blue Hills on February 15, 1832. He was thirty-four years of age.

The neighboring property was Sumner Farm when John Box Bronsdon lived there. On March 4, 1776, it was from the Sumner property that trees were cut, hidden, and moved to Dorchester Heights to reinforce the coast, helping defeat the British.

The Eustis family was very friendly and generous. W. E. C. Eustis, as he was known, came from a wealthy southern background. His grandfather was a military officer and later secretary of state, winning elections over John and Sam Adams. His father was a military general who had sold a plantation and land before he died.

This was a regular stop for Mamie's carriage, and she enjoyed coming here and shuttling the family, and she also became friendly with the people who worked for them. They had a domestic Irish cook, Mrs. Kelley, whose coffee was extraordinary, and she made Irish soda bread better than any other, even Mamie's mother's. When she baked her bread, she would bake extra loaves for a few friends. Mamie was on her list. Visiting with Miss Kelley also gave Mamie an opportunity to speak with an Irish brogue, as she fondly remembered her own parents. She would tell Mary of news she had from home in County Cork. Mary's father, James, had come from County Limerick, which neighbors Cork to its north in south-central Ireland.

Kerry Ann Kelley was raised and taught domestic life at an early age. Her father was a domestic butler, and when he saw an opportunity, Kerry was added to his staff. Young girls were trained, so at sixteen years old, she learned the life of domestic help, working her way through the various tasks. Sometimes she would be assigned to help the cook. Kerry enjoyed cooking, as she had been helping her mother since she could remember. Soon enough, the house cook asked for Kerry to become her assistant. Kerry's coffee and soda bread were so good that the family requested them.

By the time she was twenty-six, she could do all types of domestic work, from cooking to sewing. Her cousins suggested she find her way to America. With her father's blessing and a little money, she set off to a new life. Kerry had a cousin who was working for a family in Boston, so she made her way to Nova Scotia, then down to Maine, and eventually to Boston.

Boston was teeming with Irish immigrants, and by asking around, she found her cousin Theresa working for a family on Commonwealth Avenue in downtown Boston. Kerry was hired with Theresa's recommendation and sent off to clean bathrooms and make beds for the Eustis family. Not long after, Kerry was asked to work in the kitchen when the cook became sick. She made her coffee and soda bread, and the job was hers.

The Eustis family stayed in Milton all summer—actually, from the beginning of May until the end of September—and Kerry had a beautiful room of her own just off the kitchen. It looked out across a big field bordered by pine forest.

Mamie and Kerry had developed a friendship, and on Sundays Mamie had just two fares on Brush Hill Road not far from the Eustis estate. They attended church at 6:00 a.m., and Mamie had them home by 8:30. After that she was off for the rest of the day. She'd go to pick up Kerry, and they would attend the 9:00 church service at Blue Hill Community Church in Readville. Kerry didn't get the day off and had to be back to prepare the noon meal.

Mamie would normally go to Annie's house for Sunday dinner. It was a tradition of sorts that Annie always prepared a big meal, and everyone had dinner there, always well attended by family and invited friends.

There were times when Kerry was preparing something like a nice beef roast. The Eustises were wealthy people who demanded nothing but the best cuts of meat. Mamie would stay and have lunch with Kerry at her invitation. This was very good beef, and Kerry was a very good cook.

Mamie had connections and friends all over the greater Boston area, especially in Milton and Quincy. One family lived in the Milton lower mills area, near the Dorchester section of Boston. Mary Bowditch Forbes was born in 1878, the same year as Mamie, and died in 1961. She was the daughter of James Murray Forbes of Milton, who was born in 1845 and died in 1937. He worked as an agent, traveling extensively in China and trading or purchasing art, furniture, plants, and many other treasured pieces, and spent summers at his house in Dark Harbor, Maine. Many items were shipped back to Milton and decorate the family home at 215 Adams Street to this day.

James's father was Captain Robert Bennett Forbes. He and his brother, John Murray Forbes, were staunch supporters of President Abraham Lincoln. During the Civil War, the captain ordered and supervised the building and commissioning of several war vessels, and they gave strong support to the African American Fifty-Fourth Regiment training at Camp Meigs.

John Murray Forbes was a political activist during the war and made what would turn out to be an important trip to England in 1863. While dining, he endured despicable talk of the North being defeated until he rebutted the talk with great zeal and silenced the room. With this outburst and the recent victory at Gettysburg, the course of the war changed, and British support of the Confederates ended.

Mary Bowditch Forbes received a penny in 1909 to commemorate Lincoln's one hundredth birthday, and that started her collecting everything she could about Lincoln. She had collected so much by 1923 that she was talking with a friend about her need for a place to display and store her extensive collection. They came up with the idea of building a replica of the cabin in which Lincoln was born in Milton. Immediately, Mary thought of a master carpenter she knew who lived in Milton, Thomas S. Murdock.

After hearing her plan and knowing that her family had the means to pay for such a request, Mr. Murdock started planning. Mary wrote to the historical society in Hodgenville, Kentucky, seeking permission to copy the structure. Once they agreed, Mary wanted Thomas to start immediately, to which he replied that he needed the details of what he was going to build. Mary suggested that he travel to Kentucky and get whatever information he needed; she would pay all expenses.

He agreed to go at once, and the next morning, after buying a new black wool overcoat, he left for Hodgenville. With his black coat and black fedora, Thomas was often mistaken for a minister, to his delight.

At the cabin he took dimensions, made sketches, and even acquired a few items for the new cabin. Upon his return to Milton, Mary chose a site and received permission to take whatever trees were necessary from the Blue Hill area. Thomas went to work felling trees, and he hand finished all his lumber with a one-hundred-year-old hewing ax.

He ordered that a six-foot-deep foundation be dug and then filled with stone for drainage and stability. This was going to be a heavy structure. When the cornerstones were laid in November 1923, a small metal box was cemented in place by one of the corners. Inside this time capsule was some clay that Thomas had brought back from Kentucky and a 1909 commemorative penny.

The Lincoln Cabin, Milton Massachusetts

Once completed in March 1924, the cabin attracted thousands of visitors. There was a special tribute on August 14 that year, including the Grand Army of the Republic with fifteen thousand in attendance. The army bugler was the same man, with the same bugle, who had played at Grant's headquarters in Washington. When he played from inside the cabin, the crowd became ecstatic with excitement.

Mamie was there with her good friend Mrs. Harriet Murdock, Thomas's wife.

Now into the 1920s, with automobiles beginning to replace the horse-and-carriage trade, Mamie still kept up some accounts who enjoyed riding with her. When she had too much free time, she would go to one of the telegraph offices and fill in when the men were sick or too drunk to work. Nobody ever knew it was Mamie tapping out the text. The man she replaced would still get paid, and he had to pay Mamie. That way, their manager didn't know any better. There were also night letters from businesses that needed to be sent overnight for the next day's delivery. Though the telephone was starting to come into use, it cost maybe five dollars to make a call, while sending the same message by telegraph to telegram was just fifty cents.

# CHAPTER 34

# Depression Strikes

THE YEAR 1924 WAS A good year, a turning point for the Rau and Bronsdon families.

Ernie and Avis had a son born in November. The Rau's stayed at 19 Hamilton Street. Ernie enjoyed being there, and Mamie would come and have coffee with Avis every morning.

Billy bought another house in the town of Sharon, not far from the trout pond that Ernie had shown him near the sawmill. Billy and Annie used the house in Sharon for summers at first, though he still drove down to the livery daily.

The telephone was now beginning to replace the telegraph. It also began to replace Billy's system of slips for picking up freight. The orders could be called in by telephone.

Jackie had a job as a mechanic in Readville, so he remained there.

Freddy stayed in Readville, on the first floor of Annie's triple-decker.

There were always two small rooms on the first floor with just a bed, a small table, and a chair with a water pitcher and oil lamp for any traveler who needed a place for one night. There was an outhouse about twenty-five feet from the back door. Billy was strict on one-night stays, and only someone who could pass his muster could stay there. The room was fifty cents, and a meal was a bargain at ten cents. These rooms were not for hoboes. Weather affected schedules at times, and someone could miss a connecting train and need a place to stay. Billy rented the second floor to a family and kept the third floor for their own use when they wanted to be in Readville.

Mamie was still doing some of her carriage runs, but not like in the past. But she was very happy married to Jack and with good home. Though now she saw that Jack drank more than she had thought he did, or he was just plain drinking more than he had before, she kept it out of her mind and went about doing all the things that made her happy, especially visiting her friends.

Times got tough in 1929, which ushered in the Depression era. Everything became difficult. The stock market collapsed on October 29, 1929, which became known as Black Tuesday. Many lost everything they had. Hoboes on the railroad became increasingly bothersome; money and food were scarce. Billy suggested moving Avis and Paul over to Sharon for safety.

Ernie was still working at Ford, so he stayed in Readville because it was easier to get to Cambridge daily. Freddy remained in Readville taking care of the property.

Billy wouldn't live to see the Depression end. He had a heart attack on October 23, 1934. He was sixty-six years old.

CHAPTER 35

# Home in Readville

THE ECONOMIC HARD TIMES LASTED until the late thirties, but in 1935 some things began to ease, and Avis and Paul moved back to Readville.

Annie got so she preferred living in Readville during the winter months. It was nice in Sharon in the summer with the windows open and breeze blowing through. Readville was nice and felt like home, but the air smelled and felt different. It also sounded different. Annie was used to hearing the freight yard night and day. It became a normal background that was only noticeable if it stopped. Though Readville didn't feel the same without Billy, it had a comfort that Sharon did not: the feeling of Billy's presence.

There were certain train schedules that were like a clock. At two in the morning, the mail train would pull into Readville. The engineer would do a short whistle to let Wendell know it was ready. Billy would always say at 2:00 a.m., "Train's in. All is well."

Snow in winter meant trains running all night to keep the tracks clear. This also meant the stable would be active early, preparing for a hard day driving.

Paul was ten years old in 1934, and Grampa Billy was just learning to enjoy his grandson when he died. His passing affected Paul very badly. He just did not understand.

The holiday season after Billy died was notably different. He had very much enjoyed Thanksgiving, and he and George Kunkel always went out turkey hunting the day before. Fowl Meadow was an ideal place to hunt. They would each get two birds, and Billy would give one to Murch. The Kunkel's had a big family for Christmas, so they needed two.

Everybody wanted to be in Readville with the great traditions that had been passed down for years. The stores in Wolcott Square were all decorated with wreaths made from the princess pine that grew all along the river bank by Paul's Bridge. Red ribbon, bows, and stunning glass ornaments hung in windows, glimmering in the sunlight.

The celebration lasted from Thanksgiving until January 7, which was the European Christmas, an English tradition.

Everyone was happier being home in Readville. Paul was attending School, a mere stone's throw from home, but he disliked it immensely. He wanted to be working with his grandfather, missing him still. He was especially close to his uncle Jackie, a favorite of Paul's.

When Billy was working in his shop doing any of numerous repairs, Paul always seemed to be there. Billy would set up the big anvil with a saddle for Paul to play riding. When he finished his work, Billy would bring out Paul's favorite horse, which was named Hawk; he was very gentile and attentive. Paul would ride him bareback around the corral while his grandfather instructed him. There were times Billy had his carriage ready to go by the barn, and he'd tell Paul to go out and bring it around front. Paul loved doing this. Depending on where he was heading, Billy might tell Paul to get his driving gloves; they were "heading up." The term was something he had started yelling to his drivers as a young man. "Head 'em up" from Billy meant he wanted the driver's horse's head up and pulling strong.

Being an outdoorsman, Billy always carried a wooden tube with a fly rod for fishing on his carriage. Some days, he would tell Paul to "Drive me to your bridge, sir," and Paul knew he meant Paul's Bridge just down the street. Billy would start out by showing Paul how to cast, but eventually Paul got distracted by frogs, and Billy focused on casting.

The stream that made up the area leading to Paul's Bridge flowed down from Hemenway Pond. Billy had been fishing here for nearly fifty years. Knowing this stream very well, he had learned that right where the water flowed into the Neponset River was an ideal spot. There were some nice brook trout, or "brookies," as they are called. They swim up the small streams looking for food. The fish would sit in deeper water, grabbing food that washed into the river, and Billy found that by casting about four feet upstream from the end and letting his fly drift out into the river, in less than an hour, he would have six or eight fish. Billy liked to gut and rinse them there in the stream to cook at home. Paul would drive them back home and run to show Annie the fish he caught with Grampa.

Billy talked with Ernie about possibly showing Paul how to shoot a BB gun he had gotten for him. This was never mentioned to Avis, but Ernie didn't mind, and Billy got excited and said he was going to teach the boy to hunt. The next day, Billy was finishing fixing an axle on a freight wagon, and Paul was right there with grease on his hands and face.

Billy said to Paul, "What say we go for a ride, my boy? Go clean that grease off behind the barn. Don't want that on my carriage."

They drove down by Paul's Bridge but didn't stop. Billy took the reins and started up Brush Hill Road and then turned right onto what seemed more like a path than a road.

This actually was a road and had been since colonial times. It was called the Burma Road Trail, and many a patriot walked or marched this road, but it was created many years before the area was settled by white men. It started in Milton by Paul's Bridge, running all the way over to Ponkapoag, which was the site of the Massachuset clan during the winter. Now somewhat overgrown and mainly used by hunters, it was swampy and lush with green grasses, trees, and bushes with flowers and berries.

Paul asked his grandfather where they were going to fish. Then Billy pulled out the BB gun, and Paul's jaw dropped. Billy proceeded to show Paul what he needed to know as if it were a .22 rifle. Then he set up some targets to shoot at. Billy always carried a pistol, but he also kept a rifle hidden under his floorboard. There was a loose board held down with a hidden peg, and when Billy pulled up on the peg, the board would slide, revealing the compartment. He kept a .22 Winchester rifle there normally, but when fowl were in season, he carried a shotgun. Those guns were ordinarily not loaded. Billy carried bullets or shells in his pocket, but his pistol was always loaded.

Paul with his new BB gun and Billy with his .22 went walking down the path looking for rabbits. It wasn't bird season, and Billy liked eating fried rabbit. They found a rabbit eating just next to the river, and Billy told Paul that was a good spot because the rabbit couldn't run away. Then he told Paul the rabbit was facing upriver and would run straight ahead by instinct. He said to aim for the tip of its nose.

With the snap of the BB gun startling the rabbit, it did just what Billy said, because the BB hit the creature directly in the left eye. Billy was more excited than Paul and exclaimed, "Got him!"

Paul just stood looking and thinking that it was not a good thing he had done. Billy told Paul to watch carefully while he field dressed the rabbit. Paul threw up, and the pair went home.

This would be their last hunting trip before his grandfather's death.

The country was now in a full depression. Some felt the impact more than others, but everyone was affected.

Ernie and his family were getting by pretty well living in the Bronsdon house, and he was able to keep working at Ford Motor. He had an old Ford automobile, but gas was scarce; getting it was all about who you knew. The Bronsdon name having many friends and connections around the area, made gasoline readily available.

Ernie's mother, Edith, had access to a summer home on Cape Cod in Wellfleet through her family. Having transportation, Ernie would drive to the cape, which in 1932 was a major trip that took all day. The hills weren't steep, but the auto would not make some of them without enough speed. Sometimes he would have to drive in reverse up the hill, giving the car more power.

The cottage in Wellfleet was small but right on a beach close to the harbor. Next door lived a fishing captain. He was grumpy and loud, but he was always giving Edith fresh fish.

Ernie would eat plates full of oyster's right out of the water by the cottage. He even planted a garden for Edith, mainly some tomato and cucumbers. The plants grew pretty well; he brought a bucket of his soil with him anytime he went to Wellfleet. Nothing grew there like what he was used to back in Readville. The soil was very sandy and high in salt from the ocean, but you could walk some areas and find big patches of wild asparagus.

Cape Cod, we are told, was first seen by the Pilgrims in 1620 after they landed on what is now Provincetown. There is now more evidence that the Norse or Vikings were on Cape Cod by 1007, but not to settle.

In 1524 a French explorer took harbor there temporarily, as did a Portuguese ship sailing under Spanish flag in 1525. It is written that, in 1602, Bartholomew Gosnold, an Englishman, named this peninsula Cape Cod. Samuel de Champlain charted the harbor areas about 1606, Henry Hudson ventured ashore in 1609, and Captain John Smith noted it on his map in 1614. There may have been others before them. The first actual settlement on Cape Cod was established around 1640 in Nauset. The settlers came by ship and were able to find abundant fish for food, but these people were not fishermen; they were farmers. They set out to plant fields, but they soon found that the area was not suited to most crops they tried to grow, and they had to find some that would adapt. Eventually, they learned that they could grow some food and fruit, but to live there, they needed to use what the ocean offered in abundance.

Not far from Nauset was an area called Billingsgate, and in 1666 this became Wellfleet. It had a good harbor for sailing ships, and there was soon a small fleet of everything from whalers to cod boats, and the settlers learned to survive.

They observed what appeared to be a natural occurrence of whales and dolphins beaching themselves. Then they watched the natives harvesting meat and blubber for rendering oil. Once they saw the whales being led to shallow water and slaughtered in abundance, the industry flourished. This quickly depleted another resource, trees for making fires to boil down the blubber for oil.

Wharves were established, and ships were regularly sailing out and returning with great catches of cod and mackerel. Smart entrepreneurs harvested salt from the nearby salt ponds for preserving the fish. Shellfish were found in huge quantities, and soon ships were delivering fresh oysters to ports along the East Coast.

From 1920 through 1933, Prohibition was in effect. Alcohol was outlawed, which resulted in bootlegging and the corruption of wealthy investors and crooked politicians. Others were able to cash in on this lucrative endeavor as well, like Edith's sea captain neighbor Barnabas Cole. He kept an odd schedule, leaving late at night and returning by noon and always bringing home fish to give to his thankful neighbors. Some were also customers for the whiskey the captain was bringing ashore covered over by his catch. Most of what he brought in was already long gone, taken for distribution by the men that paid him. They would make a fortune in bootlegging.

There were comical acts and radio shows to entertain people during these hard times, trying to take their minds off hunger and being without. The Three Stooges were new and traveled to various cities to do shows. Ernie could not stand this kind of acting, and forbade Paul to listen to it.

Later came Ish Kabibble, another dimwitted act who would bring out some German from Ernie's father's time. Ernie often said, "Ish Kabibble in the feeble housing," especially if he was angry. This meant that Ish Kabibble belonged in the nut house; he was looney. When I was little, my father would say that just to make me laugh. He'd also tell crazy army stories from World War II.

# CHAPTER 36

# Bones, Religion, and Turmoil

PAUL WENT OUT FOR RECESS at school, jumped a fence, and ran up near the train depot where he knew Jackie would be working. Finding Jackie, he begged him not to make him go back to school; he wanted to help his uncle. Jackie talked him into going back to the school and helped smooth things over with his teacher.

Avis never found out, at least that anyone knows of.

Not long after, when Paul was twelve, he fell from one of the wagons while playing. He broke his right arm pretty badly and had a full cast from shoulder to fingers. It was very painful and caused Paul and Avis to lose much sleep. When they went back to the doctor to see how it was doing, he decided it was not healing properly. Dr. Griever decided it needed to be rebroken and set again. This time the bone did heal, but Paul couldn't straighten his arm properly. Mamie came up with the idea of strapping a weight to his hand and having Paul walk around with the weight. With the weight pulling his arm back down, the muscle and elbow joint responded, and the arm healed after about three months.

When deliveries were going to the Johnsons in Milton, Paul always wanted to go with whoever was driving that day. The Johnsons, who were wealthy and lived in a big house on Brush Hill Road, had two children, both a little younger than Paul. Their father was hardly ever home, at least from what Paul could see. The children told him their father was always working.

Mr. Howard Deering Johnson was hard at work building what would become an empire.

The Johnson children had a horse of their own but didn't care much for that type of activity, so when Paul asked if he could walk their horse, they happily let him. When Mr. Johnson saw him with the horse, he asked if Paul would like to earn some money. Paul said yes, and Mr. Johnson told him that if he brought up two bags of coal per week, he would make twenty-five cents per bag. Paul agreed, and when he told his uncle, Jackie came back the next day with a small four-wheel wagon and pull handle. He told Paul, "You are now in the freight business, buddy boy," and they both smiled.

When he started delivering the coal, Paul asked if he could walk the horse while he was there. That was fine by the Johnsons. The horse was actually a painted pony called Paint, but to Paul, it was a horse. Not long after he began walking the pony, he started riding it. He could tell this horse was happy to be out and about getting good exercise. When Paul came up the drive to deliver his coal, Paint would move right over to the gate to wait for him, and Paul would pull out an apple he had brought for his friend.

Paul's father had an adopted sister, Theresa Getchell, who was actually Edith's younger sister. Soon after their parents died, leaving the girl an orphan, Edith adopted her. One year younger than Ernie, she went by the name Pearly or Olive. She was a very religious young Catholic girl. She would leave to join a convent and fulfill her dream of becoming a nun. Pearly was already gone when Paul was born, but once she graduated and became a Dominican Sister of Peace, she was able to travel home again from Kentucky. She was now known as Sister William Teresa, William being her grandfather's name.

Everyone was very proud of Pearly.

She prayed to Saint Teresa of Avila, the patron saint of people who suffer headaches. Her feast day is October 15.

There were times in the 1960s when Sister was stationed in South Boston, and we would visit her. She played piano for us; it was fun. She came to Readville one time around 1965 with another nun and a priest. They were going down to Plymouth sightseeing and asked if I wanted to go. I went. We stopped at a restaurant to eat. When they were asked if they wanted cocktails, they ordered what sounded good. They were really surprised that their cocktails had alcohol in them. They were expecting something like shrimp cocktails.

Sister was later stationed in Brockton, and we saw her a bit more. She remained in Kentucky in her elder years, and Sister William Theresa died July 1, 1992, at the age of ninety-two. She is buried in Kentucky.

When Paul grew to his teens and got to know his aunt, it made him feel very religious. On his trips to the Johnsons' to deliver coal, Paul would walk by the seminary of the Columban Fathers in Milton near Paul's Bridge. He would watch the young seminary students as they walked quietly, studying their prayer books. Paul thought how peaceful they looked and began thinking he wanted to be a priest. At thirteen years old, he needed to talk to someone about this. He went down to Mamie and Jack's house, hoping to talk to Mamie.

She wasn't there. It was September, and Jack was collecting potatoes. He said that Mamie should be home soon and asked Paul to grab a basket and start putting in potatoes. They went about filling four bushel baskets, and Paul asked Jack what he thought about Pearly the nun. Jack said, "She's a very nice young woman from what I've seen, but too much church for my liking." Paul didn't say anything else about her to Jack.

Mamie was surprised to see Paul when she got home, and he asked to talk with her. Jack took his pipe out and lit it, and then while wiping his brow and he motioned with his pipe for Mamie to take him into the house. She said that she needed to get cleaned up and get dinner going. "So come on in the kitchen with me."

Jack said, "Thanks for the hand. Have one of her cookies for me."

Mamie asked if Paul wanted to stay for supper; she was making squab. Paul knew from experience that meant she was going to kill some pigeons, and he said no, he had homework to do. But he did get to talk to her, telling her he thought he wanted to join the Columban Fathers seminary. Without flinching but quietly shocked, she hesitated and said, "Well, this is a bit unexpected."

Then Mamie said she drove by the seminary daily and knew some of the priests who taught there. Maybe he could take a ride with her to talk to them. Paul thanked her, and off home he went. She went out to Jack and told him.

He again lit his pipe and said, "Be careful, my dear."

She knew this was not something she could undertake on her own with Avis. Early the next morning, she went to catch Ernie before he left for work to have a talk with him. Mamie worked things out in her mind while driving her carriage before moving forward. She and Ernie were close, so she knew she could talk to him, but she missed him by a minute or two. Finally, she caught up with him in the garden picking the last of his tomatoes, and she started helping as they discussed a fishing trip he was planning for Sunday afternoon.

Then Mamie said, "Yup, Sunday's a good day to go and pray you catch fish," and they both laughed.

Then she brought up what was on her mind, and at first Ernie just stood and stared at Mamie. She told Ernie that Paul had gotten this idea because of Sister Pearly. She said, "Remember years back who it was who delivered you to my sister with kid-glove hands."

They both smiled now, and Ernie thanked her and said, "Come in the house with me. You can help me with your niece." Now only Mamie laughed. Ernie was turning red and beginning to sweat as they walked to the house.

Once in the house, the first thing Ernie wanted was a cup of coffee. Avis had a pot on, and without anyone asking, she got two cups and poured them some. Both of them took a sip of coffee and looked at each other. The coffee was old and bitter.

Mamie, with an *ahh*, said, "Still got the touch, Avis," and smiled.

Then Ernie started telling her why they had come in, and she sat with them, thinking they were playing a prank on her as they often did. But no, Mamie said they were serious. "You two might want to talk to him."

Mamie was around often, so they talked the next morning, and Mamie told them that she knew a few seminarians and could just stop by there with Paul to see how it went. They all agreed, and later that day, Mamie picked Paul up from school. They drove up past Paul's Bridge. She had a fare to pick up in Milton as well.

She drove into the seminary yard just as Father Chase was walking to the chapel. He stopped and greeted them, knowing Mamie as Mary. Then he asked what she needed. Mamie introduced Paul, and he asked them to walk with him to the chapel. As they did, Mamie told him why they had stopped. Father said nothing, as they were just walking into the chapel. With ritualistic movements, the priest went to one knee and said some words that must have been Latin. Walking to the altar, he knelt, speaking more Latin. Then he sat on a bench and turned to Paul, saying, "You have a good saintly name. Let me hear your Latin."

Staring straight ahead, Paul said he couldn't speak Latin. The priest smiled and said how surprised he would have been if Paul had spoken it. "We as priests have to learn this ancient language. It is the word of the Lord." Then Father Chase asked where Paul's parents were, and Mamie explained the background of Paul's and why she brought him by. Then he asked if they went to church every Sunday. Both Paul and Mamie said yes at the same time. Father Chase invited them and their family to eight o'clock Mass Sunday there in the chapel. They could talk then.

The following Sunday, they got dressed up, and Ernie drove to the seminary in his Ford Model S for Catholic Mass, which in those days was all in Latin. After Mass, Father Chase came back to talk to the family, and he was very nice about the matter, explaining that Paul could not be an active seminarian until he was eighteen. But he could become an altar boy and begin studying Latin. "You will know if this life is for you," he said. "It will call you."

Paul went to the seminary regularly and helped with Mass, trying to learn Latin. This was really difficult to apprehend. But he was trying his best.

CHAPTER 37

# Trouble Brewing

Now it was 1939, and war in Europe was breaking out, with a madman named Adolph Hitler threatening to take over the world. He was coming to power and storming neighboring countries with force. Turmoil would escalate quickly in Asia, with Japan fiercely attacking China and wiping out the people in genocide fashion. In the late summer of 1939, with Germany invading Poland and marching across Europe at an alarming rate, France and the United Kingdom declared war. Over the next two years, Germany would extend its reach to almost all of Europe, forming an alliance with Italy and then Japan. Together, the three countries became known as the Axis. They were destructive and brutal.

Germany then moved toward the Soviet Union in Russia and annexed Finland and the Baltics. In the summer of 1941, the Axis made attempts to invade the Soviet Union in historic battles. Germany also began advancing its campaign into Africa.

With war raging in Europe, China, and now Africa, on December 7, 1941, Japan brutally attacked the United States in Pearl Harbor, Hawaii. On December 10, 1941, Germany and Italy declared war on the United States. World War II was now officially underway, as the Allied forces around the world prepared for battle.

The United States responded as it had done since colonial times. Boston's population of citizens and immigrants wanted to be part of this country. Men and women, young or old—everyone was needed. Boston had hundreds of factory buildings, and they would be valuable for manufacturing munitions.

Women would be trained in electrical work, along with welding and riveting ships together.

From downtown Boston to Hyde Park and into Readville with its busy freight yard and access to shipping freight cars of munitions for the war, the number of men who had gone to war was staggering. Women had to step up, and they did by the thousands, from working in shipyards and munition factories to being nurses and soldiers. More than two million followed the call to arms and did work that only men had ever done.

The government formed the War Manpower Commission to ensure labor was controlled to support the war effort most effectively. Factories and mills worked to support the effort. Companies that had been building machinery were now building bombs and other necessities for the military. Everything was rationed—gasoline, sugar, butter, coffee, and even meat. Every kind of metal was needed for the war effort.

The next situation came after Japan bombed Pearl Harbor. The Japanese went after all the rubber-producing plantations in the Pacific region, which supplied the United States with 90 percent of its raw material for the rubber industry.

After the unprecedented attack on Pearl Harbor, many began to worry that the US mainland might be vulnerable as well. The government issued orders that all house windows be covered in black cloth so light from indoors could not be seen outdoors.

Three-quarters of a vehicle's headlights were to be blocked out for night driving. These were very dark days for this country even more pronounced with no gas lights and most people just stayed indoors at night. This made winter seem extra-long and by 3:30 in the afternoon the sun goes down early that time of year. Everyone would huddle around the radio at night to hear the news from Europe and Pacific. Praying for this to be over soon.

# CHAPTER 38

# John and Apolonia, Immigration

THE MAN BILLY REFERRED TO as his "German friend" was John Anufrom, a farmer in Dedham. He lived in an area that was called the Manor. John had a fairly big family and was pretty strict about hard work and always trying harder.

Dedham, Massachusetts, bordered by Boston, was one of the first towns settled as a defense against Indian attack in 1635. It was protected by rivers, a great swamp, and an open plain. Concord was settled as a western defense against attack. The area around Dedham was fertile, and farms soon dotted the countryside. The southernmost area of what would eventually be a town was Sprague Farm, which later became known as the Manor, an area bordered by the railroad to the east, Hooper Hill to the west, Sprague Pond to the north, and thick, boggy woods to the south. Hooper Hill is actually the section of Sprague Street running down from the Capen School and then turning right onto Hooper Road and going down to the railroad tracks. This small section was about two hundred acres and had very fertile soil from many years of grazing animals. There doesn't seem to be a clear reason for the name Manor; it may have just developed over time.

John and Apolonia emigrated from Eastern Europe at different times and from different situations and countries. John, my grandfather, was born in Zoskly, Lithuania, on July 24, 1886.

Vintage Statue of Liberty photo

From 1863 to 1917, Lithuania was struggling for autonomy from Poland, while at the same time the Russians were practicing what was called Russification. Forcing these smaller countries to give up their culture and language for Russian. There was anti-Catholic dissent against Lithuanians, and a political map of the region placed Lithuania as part of the Russian Empire. Then in 1904, the abolition of the Lithuanian press stimulated a revolution that would last another thirteen years.

John Boleslov Anufrom would leave his homeland in 1900 for a new life in America, arriving as a teenager of fifteen. John grew up quickly in this new world. The years that followed were filled with turmoil in Lithuania and eventually war when the Nazis invaded. John was not an educated man; in fact he had never gone to school at all. But he'd learned much working on farms, raising and slaughtering animals. Growing vegetables was as normal to him as washing his hands. It was the way things were.

Apolonia Kudryk was born on September 6, 1895, in Jezierna, Ukraine, a beautiful country with mountains, forests, rivers, and lakes. But the area was in conflict, and all of Eastern Europe was considered Galicia or Ruthenia, with Russia across the border. World events had escalated by 1914, and at age nineteen, Apolonia and a friend found themselves aboard the ocean liner *Bismarck*. On February 10, 1914, they sailed for America and the port of Boston to begin a new life. Apolonia's father had given her some money to get started. She found a place to live in a boarding house not far from Boston Harbor.

Soon she found work doing housekeeping to pay room and board at the same location. The area was called the West End of Boston. This section was populated by people of many backgrounds and ethnicities. There were many Jews from areas around Eastern Europe who brought their craft of preparing food for the delicatessens that were everywhere.

Around the turn of the twentieth century, the North End was overflowing with forty thousand immigrants. At that time events were unfolding because of World War I. Immigration from Eastern Europe swelled, and the Boston population grew to as much as ninety thousand people, expanding into the West End.

While attending church, Apolonia formed some friendships, and they all helped one another get established in America. Polly, as she was called, became great friends with Mrs. Anna Piecewicz, who lived in South Boston at 35 Prebble Street. This area of South Boston was ethnic Polish, Lithuanian, and Ukrainian. The neighborhood around Prebble Street was clearly European, with groceries, meats, and delicatessens stocking foods that were common at home.

Eventually, John began working as a porter in the West End near Apolonia's boarding house. He'd see her walking about in the area and didn't hesitate to approach her. After he introduced himself, they went to a local shop for coffee.

During these times young men and women from afar needed to establish a family here and have children. Soon after meeting John, Apolonia was sending a letter back home asking her father, Peter, for some money to be married.

John was strong, smart, and able, and he could speak English well with a slight accent. He was able to find better work. Working seven days a week was normal for the immigrant population in America, and John was living the dream.

The North End of Boston was cramped but necessary as ethnic groups stayed together for protection. It was a melting pot of people from different countries and backgrounds. Everybody had to eat, and the only way to survive was hard work.

The city of Boston was congested and filthy. Garbage was everywhere. But the North End was exceptionally dirty, with all its tenements filled with people, some families of ten living in space for three. Odors from rotting garbage and raw sewage were common.

Shopping was a daily task, and the area near Faneuil Hall was the local market, with pushcarts selling everything from meat to cheese, vegetables, and fish. Immigrants from different countries established farms, they learned to grow their own produce and fruits then came here to sell their wares. Both John and Polly felt a connection to home in Eastern Europe when at the market area, with the smell of fruits and vegetables, some ripe and delicious, others a bit past. But it all came together to create its own environment. This smell and the market event would continue on for decades, and Haymarket Square is still there.

# CHAPTER 39

# The Anufroms in America

ON JULY 25, 1915, JOHN and Apolonia were married in Boston. Living in Cambridge, they began their new family. George, the oldest, was born on June 17, 1916. Helen was born on February 6, 1918. During the time John was building a new house in Woburn, Apolonia was carrying another child. Joseph was born on September 12, 1919, while they were still living in Cambridge.

They ran into some financial problems and lost the Woburn house before it was finished. With another child about to be born, the family needed more space. Not just a house—an area with room to grow food and raise some livestock. Then on June 4, 1921, they were blessed with another son, Charles.

John had heard of an area with land available, but it was quite a way from the city, and Polly was just getting used to its hustle and bustle. But this was an opportunity they would pursue.

John and Apolonia Anufrom were used to hard work, having immigrated from so far away. They were young and strong. They built a new life in a sparsely populated section of the town of Dedham, with lots of field area for growing vegetables and raising a hog or two each year. Their new home might be away from the city, but it was beautiful, and the family quickly got established.

Sophie, their first child to be born in Dedham, arrived on August 30, 1923. Then came Stella, born on September 12, 1925. Lillian, born on August 30, 1927, would be my mother. Sophie and Lilly, besides having the same birthday, would share a special bond that lasted a lifetime. Another son, Walter, was born on August 19, 1929. He would be too young for World War II, still an adolescent.

The war in Europe took most men into active service in 1941. Now help from women of all ages and skill levels was needed in places like the Boston Naval Shipyard and the Watertown Arsenal, which manufactured munitions for the war effort. News from overseas was horrible. This was world war, but to John and Polly, there was a personal level. They had left family there some years ago.

John and Apolonia were busy twenty-four hours a day it seemed, especially with cooking. They had eleven children. Their oldest son, George, was twenty-five and signed right up for military service. Joe and Charlie soon followed, fighting the Japanese in the Pacific theater. John and Polly had seven daughters; they all joined the women behind the men of World War II.

Many factories in the Boston area were converted to war-related efforts. Factories along Hyde Park Avenue that had been producing machinery and parts were retooled. Just outside of Readville and a short walk up the railroad tracks from the Manor, there were foundries and mills for many purposes. Companies that had made distilling equipment were making shell casings. Assembly lines copied the effective systems of Ford Motors. The women learned to assemble incendiary bombs and became quite good at the tedious work, sometimes working sixteen hours a day.

Polly still had two young daughters at home, and it may have been easier with fewer people in the house, but she had become used all the family being around and enjoyed it. The younger girls, who were born in the 1930s, were Florence and the youngest child in the family, Phyllis.

Polly was busier than ever; she cooked constantly. The girls would be starving before and after work, and she sent food with them to work as well. The entire country was just starting to recover from the Great Depression, and this family was used to having very little but enough to get by. Potatoes were a mainstay for them. They grew them in a huge field. Plowing, planting, and digging were all done by hand. They stored much of the produce in the dirt basement during the winter.

Chunks of salt called corns were readily available. The salt was used for preserving many food items. Beef and pork fat were salted, and codfish was preserved in salt before drying.

Mid-September would bring cooler fall temperatures, and that meant it was time to slaughter a hog. The whole family and a few good friends would work hard after slaughtering the four-hundred-pound hog right there at home in the yard. Everyone helped, and Polly used just about every bit, making sausage and grinding pork for golumpkis. Fresh blood would be mixed with barley and spices for blood sausage, Polly's favorite. Hams, shoulders, and hocks were smoked, and John used his European expertise to preserve the meats.

This was also a time for making some income. People in the area knew that John would be smoking and would hire him to smoke meats they brought for curing. John also knew how to make pastrami using brined flat-cut beef brisket, the meat at the flat cut of the fatty section where the cow's navel would be. This cut is best for a pastrami.

Polly knew the brining process from her childhood; it was used regularly in the Ukraine. She had her own spice mix and left the brisket to soak for four to six weeks in the salty, spicy liquid. The next step was very important. Being well salted, the meat was safe for a short period. John would hang it for half a day to dry a bit and let the salt form a layer for the smoke to adhere to. Then the meat would go into the smoker overnight or until John had what he was looking for; he learned from experience.

Polly would steam the meat, setting it in a pan of water, covered, and braising it in a slow oven for four to six hours. After it came out and rested, it sliced perfectly for a sandwich on her delicious potato rolls.

When the weather was cold, from about November till March, John would keep a small, smoky fire in the smokehouse to help preserve other meats and fish and retard spoilage a bit longer. The smoke kept bacteria from forming. Mackerel and bluefish were John's favorite fish in season, and trout was plentiful.

Two Saturdays a month, John and Polly would go to the Haymarket in Boston. Pushcarts laden with produce and seafood would be set up all around Faneuil Hall. Men sold meats, cheese, and butter from the cool-storage basement of the building. Discarded vegetables and rotted fruits were all over the streets. Hawkers would be barking out what they had to sell. Competition was rampant, and bargains were many as goods exchanged hands for cash. Live and cooked crabs and fresh fish were kept on ice. Oysters were shucked and eaten, or they could be had by bushel basket.

John and Polly would buy some beef or lamb and always a big round of Muenster cheese. The whole family would feast when they got home.

They also kept a large henhouse producing eggs and meat birds as needed. Walter was in charge of selling the eggs from a corner in East Dedham Square. He also delivered to some regular customers along the Manor.

Polly was not a big woman, but she was strong, and with her family, the need for food was continuous. Without modern conveniences like refrigeration, she had to be creative. Foods that she made in her home became her staples, as growing children need energy and calories. Rice, dry and easy to store, was very useful for filling hungry stomachs. Polly also needed to be creative in using less to make more, and she was, always adding a little Apolonia flavor, so her food had her signature taste. Her golumpki, or stuffed cabbage, were legendary and a mere peasant food made from simple ingredients.

There was always a light on in the kitchen on Hooper Road. At any given time, Polly would be there cutting, chopping, and cooking. Three in the morning could bring the scent of pork cooking as she began her stuffed cabbages. She had her own method and would tell anyone who wanted to know how to make them.

First, she diced salt pork fat, saved from the pig, and rendered it down to cracklings in a big cast-iron skillet. She added four cups of cooked rice to the cracklings, then put the rice mixture into her big clay bowl. In the pan still coated with pork fat, she cooked some diced onion; green pepper; chopped garlic; and celery, if it was available. She added that to the rice with some salt, pepper, and chopped tomato. Last would be the ground meat, normally pork, but it could be beef; at Eastertime, it might be lamb. Food was made according to what was available. Lamb was a treat for John; it really did make a golumpki taste a bit different, his favorite.

After adding the ground meat, she'd mix the entire bowl together by hand. Polly could turn this into a game to get the kids to help and learn. Finally, the mixture had to be rolled in steamed cabbage leaves and stacked into a huge pan to roast in the wood-fired oven very slowly. This would produce a stuffed pillow of meat and vegetables that just melted in the mouth, very savory with a bit of the gravy that was always on the stove.

There was freshly cooked food around all the time, which was how Polly cooked. You would eat when you got hungry, and nobody starved. Her pierogis, made with pork fat cracklings, fried onion bits, and butter and served with sour cream, were legendary. Pies and biscuits were made with lard, and they cooked differently than a butter-based pastry dough.

Hungry mouths made for less storage.

# CHAPTER 40

# Annie's Army

ANNIE JOSEPHINE HICKEY BRONSDON DIED March 12, 1941. She developed arthritis in her knees during the latter part of the thirties, and she had gained a lot of weight after Billy died in 1934. Soon after, Annie was told she had diabetes. She completely misunderstood what she should do and just continued her routine.

Her health was getting progressively worse. Mamie saw what she was going through and tried to help.

In the summer of 1936, Annie's eyes started getting worse, and by 1938 she could barely see out of her left eye. The right eye wasn't much better, but she could still see a bit, enough to get by. By 1940 she was blind, but in her environment, she was still dignified and stoic.

Annie told Mamie that she had something on her forehead just before she passed. Mamie assumed she had a stroke, but there was no official cause of death considered at the time. From 1939 until she died, Annie never left her third-floor home. She quietly passed while seated in her favorite rocker.

By this time, the family had already started selling the freight business part and parcel. With Annie and Billy gone, nobody wanted to go into the three-decker again, and they sold it.

Avis and Ernie stayed at 19 in Readville with their family for a short time after Annie's death. Then they moved back out to Sharon to the quiet comfort of the country. Living in Sharon without all the commotion of the freight business was at first very different. It felt like part of life was missing.

Life in Readville was going pretty much from sunup to sundown and then some. This would have been nice to share with Annie and Billy; the family missed them very much.

With all the customers and businesses the Bronsdon brothers had done work for, Billy had made many friends, and all felt these losses as well. Jobs Billy had hired men to do, like the firewood business, were taken over by the same men. They were now a new company on their own, helping to secure an income for their families. The freight business was very different now with motorized trucks.

Billy and Annie are buried in Milton Cemetery together, and Cheryl and I were there a few days ago.

By December 1941, Paul was quietly studying at the seminary and had become a bit of protégé to Father Chase. But the United States was now fully involved in the war, and Annie's death was on his mind. He was not used to death and secretly didn't understand why God had done this, just when he felt he was getting over his grandfather's death. Barely seventeen years old, Paul was still in his senior year at Hyde Park High School, but the military would take you with one parent's signature.

He talked to both Avis and Ernie. His mother was against it, since he had just turned seventeen and was of average height but scrawny, barely weighing 115 pounds. Ernie thought it was the right thing. Paul was the eldest of four children. With his paperwork signed, he was soon shipped off to Fort Campbell, Kentucky, for basic training. Following basic training, he was sent to New Jersey.

Fort Monmouth was originally established for World War I, and now with World War II, the area was broken up into smaller camps with various tasks. The camp's main mission was the signal corps, and training was divided between transportation and base support. Demanding and rigorous, basic training was difficult, but everyone passed, unless something was very obvious. There was war on and everyone was needed.

Paul's uncle Herbert Rau, Ernie's younger brother, signed on at forty-two years old. He had been cooking at the Blue Bird Café for years and was now doing catering for weddings and parties. He was drafted and after basic training was sent to Africa. Assigned to a heavy armored-tank division, Herbert somehow ended up driving an officer's jeep with little skill. Not long after the assignment, while he was driving General George Patton behind his tanks, the general asked if he needed glasses because his driving was so bad. It turned out that Herbert had very poor eyesight, and Patton had him put on KP duty. He was fine cooking.

Paul had a hard time with the army food and being away from home. Once through the first part of training, the men were separated into categories. Soon they would find out where they would go, to the Pacific or European theater. Every one of these men was going to war; there was absolutely no doubt of that. Officers would decide their occupations. Everyone was trained in firing weapons as a matter of self-defense; after all, this was war.

The army found that Paul excelled at driving vehicles, and he was trained as a truck driver, which was a good job to have. Even though you were an infantryman, being a truck driver meant less walking. On July 12, 1943, Paul was issued his military driver's license at the ripe old age of nineteen.

This massive buildup of troops that began early in 1942 was now bigger than any the world had ever known. Once their training was over, the men were given leave time before they shipped out. Paul got a fourteen-day leave and had orders to be at Fort Dix in New Jersey when the fourteen days were up. He caught a train heading north. Men in uniform rode free on all trains at the time. Getting into the Readville Depot on a Tuesday morning in April, he was greeted by many familiar faces and friends also in uniform. Ernie knew he was coming in but kept it from Avis as a surprise, and a great surprise it was.

Paul arrived tired and hungry. Avis was about to make him some breakfast, but Ernie told her to sit and talk while he made some pancakes and eggs. After breakfast Paul went to his room and slept in his own bed for the next sixteen hours. The next day, they all had a nice roast chicken dinner, as Ernie had decided this was special occasion and had sacrificed a hen. Then Paul put on his uniform and headed out to see how Readville was doing.

He got together with Bud Haley and Freddy Phillips, and they headed out to a tavern on Hyde Park Avenue. The Cavern House was situated across the street from one of the factories that was manufacturing bombs and ammunition for the war. It was a little bar for socializing and drinking cold beer, and it had good food for a barroom. Bud was in uniform, too—he'd be heading to the Pacific—but Freddy Phillips was deferred from serving, as he had a job in manufacturing that was essential to the war effort. His grandfather owned Kunkel Forge, which produced train parts critical to the tens of thousands of rail cars needed just to transport troops.

The men were reminiscing about what they'd been going through, when the screaming break whistle sounded from the factory. Minutes later, the place was packed with the few men who worked at the factory and lots of women, who were the majority of its employees. Bottles of beer and Coke were being passed everywhere, and the air was thick with tobacco smoke. Spotting the men in uniform, the ladies went right to them, and Bud and Paul were no exception. Two young girls said hello to Bud, and he introduced his friends to them. One of the women said her name was Stella, and her sister was Sophie. They were on break from the factory. Sophie was just plain friendly and enjoyed talking to everybody who would listen. Stella was more interested in what her friends at the bar were up to. When the whistle blew, it was time for them to get back to work.

The days flew by, and it was time for Paul to head for New Jersey and whatever else might lie ahead. Bag packed and good-byes said, Paul rode to South Station with Ernie, who wanted to see him off.

Arriving at Fort Dix, Paul was directed to where his regiment would be staged from. On his first full day at Dix, he had multiple vaccine shots that hurt badly, and then equipment was issued and everyone was transported to the port of New York by railroad.

Hundreds of rail coaches arrived, carrying men by the thousands packed in like sardines. The *Queen Mary* had been pushed into service in 1940 and was transporting almost fourteen thousand troops to the United Kingdom on each trip. She was the largest and fastest transport ship of her day. Nicknamed "Grey Ghost," she would transport more than three-quarters of a million military personnel during the war. The Germans wanted the *Queen Mary* sunk, and Adolph Hitler put a $200,000 bounty out to any U-boat captain who could get her.

The ship, massive as it was, was packed to the gills once loaded with troops and supplies, vehicles and weapons. Sailing across the Atlantic Ocean can be a daunting trip, and Paul's journey would be memorable. There was a major storm just before the halfway point, and the ship rolled and listed. The waves were so big, the ship rode up and back down. There was saltwater coming right over her nose, and almost everyone was seasick. Paul was as sick as anyone; he felt like he was turned inside out, and this wouldn't stop until he got off the ship.

They hit another storm just as they arrived at the English Channel, and it was deemed too dangerous to try and dock, so they stayed at sea for a day and a half, waiting out the storm.

Once docked, the troops were unloaded and the ship emptied. She would return to New York and do the trip again many times over the coming years.

The men were sent to various locations around England and Scotland. Training would be constant. Barracks were long and built low and in a hurry. There were cots to sleep on, and food was supplied by the British, consisting mainly of mutton, or old sheep. Paul had a really hard time with the meat; it tasted spoiled to him, and as bad as his mother's cooking was, he was wishing for it now.

Training was the daily activity. No one knew what was coming, but they trained for it. Months passed, and a plan was made. The Allies would simultaneously invade from three positions, with the beach at Normandy, France, the main focus.

They needed light from a full moon, and the tide would be extra high because of the moon's phase. The higher tide would bring the transports closer to shore. On June 6, 1944, D-day, thousands of men and tons of equipment would mobilize for the invasion of Normandy.

After many delays, General Eisenhower decided they had to go ahead even with poor conditions. The Germans were comfortable that the weather would not support an attack and let down their defenses, and many went off on leave.

There were paratroopers landing all over France, and some were being sent in as decoys to get the Germans to defend the wrong section. The ploy did work to some degree, but the beaches of France were red with blood, and there was tremendous loss of life. However, this would prove to be a turning point in the war.

The Allied forces defeated the Axis, and May 8, 1945, was officially the end of the war in Europe. The Japanese finally surrendered on September 2, 1945.

The troops came home, and the United States was in for a boom time of celebrating and rebuilding.

# CHAPTER 41

# Postwar Vacation

THE YEARS BEFORE WORLD WAR II were brutal economically for the entire country, but then the war put another spin on life. Many lives were lost, and Europe was devastated by bombs, bullets, and blood; death was everywhere. But that war did something to America and the way the entire country pulled together along with our allies to defeat the Axis powers. They were forced to an all-out, unconditional surrender.

Slowly at first and region by region, cities and towns were regaining the life that had changed so drastically. Factories that produced bombs and ammunition were transformed back to other manufacturing opportunities, and there were lines of men wanting jobs. Ernie had kept working at Ford Motor through all those rough years, but to say he was just lucky would be an understatement. Any man who could pass a fairly simple physical had been sent to war. This left a workforce of mostly unqualified men and women. The women came to build cars, and Ernie was smart enough to roll with the job. He would show anyone who needed help how to do whatever needed to be done. Together, they found easier ways to accomplish things that men had always done, like lifting heavy objects. Ford Motor took notice, and Ernie worked his way up in management.

While working in the Somerville plant, Ernie became friendly with another supervisor who invited him down to his cottage in Carver for July Fourth weekend. The Fourth fell on a Sunday that year, and his friend Barney suggested he take Friday off and head down Thursday afternoon. Ernie was thrilled. He knew there would be fishing and maybe some beer and hot dogs.

When he got home, Avis was cooking dinner. He laid out the plan he had. Avis, we'll say, wasn't nearly as excited as Ernie; in fact she didn't like the idea at all. Her first question was what type of facilities there would be. After telling Avis there was an outhouse, Ernie had to chase her around the kitchen to talk. Ernie had a way with situations, and he was masterful at getting what he wanted—ask Henry Ford.

The year was 1948, and the long weekend was set. From the Sunday before they would be leaving, Ernie was getting things ready. Avis got some things together, they packed up the car, and the whole tribe headed out, leaving Readville at one o'clock in the afternoon. They arrived at West Pond in Carver, right on the Plymouth line, just after five.

There were no highways yet, and roads were much different than they are today. But it was summer, and there was plenty of daylight. Barney's wife had made hot dogs and beans on a tripod hanging over the fire for the hungry group.

Ernie had brought a can of his huge night crawlers for fishing, and Barney told him about a store in North Plymouth that carried a nice assortment of fishing gear and lures. That evening, Ernie hooked an eight-pound smallmouth bass on a worm, and Barney hooked a nice eleven-pound largemouth bass on a lure from the store in Plymouth, Benny's.

The next morning, Barney took Ernie for ride down by the waterfront, which he loved. The smell alone was intoxicating and even better at low tide with the mud. Now at nine o'clock in the morning, Ernie was dying for fried clams. Barney laughed and asked if he wanted a beer with the clams as they pulled into Benny's parking lot.

This was a new experience for Ernie. Benny's was such a diverse store having fishing gear, garden tools, automotive parts and household goods and Ernie was not one to shop. He was a buyer; he knew what he wanted and was done. Not so here. With rows of lures, rods, reels, and nets, it was his kind of variety store.

Beginning the next year, 1949, Ernie was able to make deal with Barney that he could use the cottage for two weeks during the summer. This was just a camp. Barney lived up in Jamaica Plain in a big brick house near Jamaica

Pond. West Pond would become a regular place the family would use for several years.

That first full two weeks in 1949 were a learning experience; a weekend and two weeks were very different. Living in Readville, necessities like gasoline were readily available. That first year, Ernie ran out twice. The first time was the worst. When he was just leaving to go to Plymouth, the car died. Ernie knew why right away and was steaming mad. He walked an hour and a half to the center of Carver where he found Carmichael's gas station, really just a white house with a set of stairs leading inside and one pump out front, twenty cents a gallon. Ernie was happy to find gas, and after he told his story, the attendant let him use a can. After filling the can, Ernie said he'd only been paying seventeen cents a gallon at home. The attendant asked if that included a ride back to his car for the three cents. While riding back, the man asked what Ernie did for work. He thought it funny that a man who built cars would run out of gas.

The second time they were in Plymouth again, out to get steamer clams. Ernie knew the sound his car made as it was about to run out of gas. By chance there was a gas station on his right, and he coasted up to the pump, nobody the wiser.

The same year, Paul and Lillian had a daughter stillborn. Ernie and Avis had the camp to themselves in 1950 with Rita, young Avis, and Ernie Jr.

Paul and Lillian were invited down as well. They had three-year-old Beth with them, and Ernie had heard about a new attraction in Carver. A cranberry grower had set up a train for harvesting his vast acreage of cranberries. He was trying to make some money when the train was not in use to help offset the expense.

They all had a picture taken on the first train ride as the Edaville Railroad was about to depart with twenty-two passengers, sixteen of whom were in Ernie's group.

Ernie's first stop each year was Benny's for his lures and the lobster pound for steamers, his favorite. He loved the steaming liquid from the pot, calling it "the liquor" and drinking it by the cupful.

They would have a big lobster boil with a huge pot Barney kept at the cottage. It was as big as a trash can with a drain pipe near the bottom. Ernie had a

method using a wire basket he had from the Ford plant for cleaning parts. He could fill the wire basket and lower it down so he didn't have to fish around the big pot later. The spigot was used to get cups of broth and to empty the pot. Potatoes went on the bottom and started ten minutes before the onions, sausage, and corn on the cob. Next the steamers went in with the lobsters on top for about thirty minutes, and the whole thing was ready. Lots of melted butter and napkins were set up on a long table, and Ernie invited those in the neighboring cottages to have some.

This became a yearly event.

CHAPTER 42

# Mamie and Jack 1941–1957

MAMIE AND JACK MCDONOUGH WERE in their sixties in 1941. They were in better shape than many during the Depression, and now with Japan attacking Pearl Harbor, they were going back into war again. Both had lived through World War I and the devastating effects of that period. The Depression was bad, but even then, they were somewhat shielded from the worst effects of that period.

Finding any money, food, and a place to live were the hardest part of the Depression. But Jack grew enough to feed them, and the bounty of the land had game and birds readily available to them. They had a nice, comfortable house, and Jack owned quite a bit of land, holding the deeds and keeping up with the property tax. Most of his holdings were adjacent to his house, and quite a bit of it was garden. The garden sustained them very well and even produced some minor income, or at least things to barter, as everybody needed food. There was hunting right out toward Blue Hill. Pigeons and poultry were a ready supply of meat.

Automobiles were now the main form of transportation, with many restrictions during wartime. The McDonough's still kept a horse and wagon; it was normal to them. Besides, gasoline was being rationed, with very little available outside the military.

There was still plenty to do living in rural Readville. Most of the daily chores were routine for Mamie these days. And there was early-morning coffee while taking in the sights and smells of their Readville oasis. This was a very special and unique experience for Jack and Mamie, being just a few miles from the city. Jack had experienced mornings here for years and loved his place. Mamie being here made it something far better than he had known.

Jack designed and made birdhouses of stones and cement, building them like small castles. He attracted pheasants and peacocks by putting bit of food or seed in the houses; they were Mamie's pals.

Sitting on the stoop of Jack's old front step, this big piece of granite that just somehow stayed when the new house was built, they'd enjoy the view of Blue Hill gradually sloping down to the meadow, tree lined with no other houses invading the view. The meadow area turned brown as the reeds of cat-o'-nine-tails would dry in the fall. When water was abundant, the meadow would fill, and the view would be bright blue when the sky was clear, creating a spellbinding reflection with the contrast of green grasses, blue water, and brown reeds. Waterfowl were abundant. Jack could easily carry his canoe close enough to get in the water for an easy duck hunt. He and Mamie liked to smoke the duck using applewood. Squirrels were hand fed. Jack's spaniel, Corky, wasn't happy with the squirrels but kept a distance.

Mornings after breakfast at six o'clock, Jack, even in his sixties, drove his wagon out along the tracks as he'd done for years. Mamie was amazed how many things he found that had somehow fallen off the railcars.

Mamie was enjoying her time at what they referred to as "Fowl Meadowview." It was quiet and convenient to Boston. She became a devoted letter writer to Paul, Freddy, and a few others in the service. Every Tuesday, Mamie would write her letter and be sure it was sent by Thursday. She put together care packages, sending one a month but not knowing if they made it or not. She would make cookies and had Jack make her some small wooden boxes to keep them from being crushed.

Readville was a hidden jewel, but Mamie's Readville was like a treasure chest. Most of the area away from the train station down to the meadow was still sparsely populated. The only listings near Jack and Mamie in the 1920 census were Mamie's cousins the Hickeys and the Kunkel's. Between the twenties and thirties, all the land around them that Jack owned was transferred over to Mamie by attorney Harry Dean.

The house was big, but with just two people, it was easy to keep clean, and Mamie kept a very clean house. Many hours were passed in the kitchen. In the colder months, with the wood-fired cookstove, Mamie used the benefit of a hot oven to bake while heating the house. In the spring and summer, the windows were almost always open, and there would be a breeze off the meadow and a view up to Blue Hill.

Years before, just after Mamie and Jack were married, he had a deed drawn up dated April 1, 1925, for the area of six lots on and around Chester and Forest Streets containing almost one acre. The lots were all pre-established with the Norfolk County Registry of Deeds on January 20, 1896, by H. T. Whitman, surveyor.

Jack continued drinking his whiskey and was a heavy smoker—pipe, cigar…he smoked them all. Eventually, the smoking caught up with him, and he developed a very bad cough and was always extremely congested. When Mamie was finally able to get him to go to a doctor, the diagnosis was not good. The smoking had caused cancer in his throat and larynx, which was eventually removed at Massachusetts General Hospital. Mamie was right there to help Jack day and night, taking care of him as best she could.

Harry Dean, Esquire, a close friend of both Jack and Mamie, had handled all their legal doings, and now it was time for a will. The only thing Jack cared about was that Mamie be taken care of and have a place to live. Harry got it all together, and Mamie was Jack's sole beneficiary, though he did have Mamie put four hundred dollars in an account managed by his nephew Peter in Quincy for any expenses Henry might have. The property around Readville, including Mamie and Jack's bungalow, was put in Mamie's name. Jack sold some lots to help with expenses.

Late in 1957, Jack succumbed to the disease and passed away. His funeral was December 14, 1957, and he was buried in Quincy Cemetery. Interesting fact: Cheryl and I would be married seventeen years later to the day: December 14, 1974.

From a 1798 tombstone at Copp's Hill Cemetery, Boston:

Stop here my friend and cast an eye.
As you are now so once was I.
As I am now, so you must be,
Prepare for death and follow me.

After Jack passed away, Mamie was greatly affected, as her life was drastically changed. She was seventy-nine when Jack died, and he was eighty-two. These were good old ages for that time. Now, with the help of Harry Dean, she was able to put together a plan that she and Jack had discussed between themselves but had not shared with anyone else.

Mamie's favorite nephew, Paul Rau, was living in Framingham now, working at Ford Motor in Somerville, where his father, Ernie, was a supervisor. They were building Edsels. Mamie asked Paul to come and meet with her. She had an offer he couldn't refuse!

After World War II, when the troops came home, there were celebrations galore, and all the boys who left for war had come home men. They wanted to get married, raise a family, and own a home: the American dream. Developers built scores of houses, and people bought and developed neighborhoods all over the country, just like they did in Framingham.

Paul and Lillian were married March 5, 1946, and were living in Roxbury. They had an apartment in a three-decker on Valentine Street near the Mission Hill area of Boston, also known as Roxbury. On May 12, 1947, Elizabeth Ann Rau was born, and a new family began. Then in 1949 another daughter was born, but this was a stillborn baby. She was named Paula Rau and was buried in Milton Cemetery with Billy and Annie Bronsdon. A couple of years later, Susan Pauline Rau was born on June 16, 1951.

In 1956, they were living in Framingham in a new post–World War II development. This was a nice, quiet area, still rural but close to the main roadways, in a section called Nobscot Hill situated in the northeast corner by Sudbury and Wayland. It was a nice neighborhood with friendly people, and they were enjoying life. Lillian was carrying another baby as well.

We'll call it bad luck. Or maybe it was just a big bump in life's road.

The Edsel was being touted in advance of sales as being like the Green Hornet's car, Black Beauty, but it turned out to be more of a black eye, a disaster for Ford Motor. The Somerville plant closed in February 1958, severely damaging many livelihoods and causing the local economy to lose $1 million a year in taxes.

During the war in Europe, Paul had been trained as a driver. He could drive anything from motorcycles to tractor trailers, and he really loved driving the big rigs. Acquiring the proper license as a civilian after the war was very easy. He just needed his military record and a driving test, and Paul had the class-one license that he would keep forever. Soon he was driving tractor trailers over the road throughout New England and into New York for Tropicana orange juice. Although most trips were just for one night, he was away for three to five days at times. That part Lillian didn't like.

Paul came to see Mamie at her house on Chester Street in Readville, as she had requested. The family came along to visit, and while the girls played outdoors, Mamie laid out her reason for the meeting. It was more than just a visit. She was elderly and without Jack. He had left her all that he owned, and she was completely without debt. Mamie had her house on a large lot, and she had the other lots in the area. Mamie made her favorite nephew a very generous offer.

She offered Paul some of the land she now owned to build a new house for his growing family, with the stipulation that she be provided a place to live until she died. The house that she and Jack had lived in would be sold, so she would have some money to live on.

Paul and Lillian were overwhelmed. Mamie was, too, but they all knew this was a good thing for everybody.

Mamie had contacted Harry Dean about having the name of the road in front of her property facing Fowl Meadow changed. It was called Forest Street, and Mamie requested that it be changed beginning at Stanley Street, which is now Stanbro Street. From there to the old racetrack property, it would be Meadowview Road. Mamie paid $380 on April 20, 1956, to the City of Boston Public Improvement Commission.

Mr. Dean was again retained by Mamie to write her last will and testament, leaving what she wanted to the family. Mamie made Paul the executor of her will. He made sure her wishes were followed.

There were jobs galore, and Paul was doing what he liked most, driving trucks. The work at Tropicana had been good but monotonous with hours. Paul had met Al Briggs, the owner of a motor freight company in Framingham that ran straight job-style trucks, twenty-four feet, some of which had refrigeration for perishable goods. The job was driving trucks, but not tractor trailers

DRAFT for WILL of         ( Jan. 30, 1959.)
Mrs. Mary C. McDonough.

   Be it Remembered that I, Mary C. McDonough,(widow of John M.
McDonough,)
of No. 9 Meadowview Road, Readville District, Boston, Mass.

being of sound mind and memory, but knowing the uncertainty of

this life, do make this my last will and testament, hereby

revoking all former wills by me at any time heretofore made.

   After the payment of my just debts and funeral charges, I
bequeath and devise as follows:

   First. I give all the rest and residue of my property and
estate, real, personal or mixed, of every kind and nature and
wherever situated, of which I shall die seized and possessed,
or to which I shall be entitled at the time of my decease,
in equal shares, share and share alike, to
   Avis Bronsdon Rau, wife of Ernest P. Rau, of No. 108 Brush
Hill Road, Milton, Mass.,

William Cushman Bronsdon, of No. 45 West Shore Road, Holbrook, Mass.,

John Paul Bronsdon of No. 108 Brush Hill Road, Milton, Mass.,

Rita Rau Barnicle of No. 10 Circlar Avenue, Natick, Mass.,

E. Avis Rau Benassie of No. 108 Brush Hill Road, Milton, Mass. and

Ernest W. Rau of No. 108 Brush Hill Road, Milton, Mass.

to them and their heirs absolutely.

   Second. If John Paul Rau Senior should predecease me I give all

of the real estate which I conveyed to myself and said John Paul Rau,

Senior, as Joint Tenants and not as Tenants in Common, by a Deed dated

April 12, 1958, recorded with Suffolk Deeds in Book 7304 page 244

of Suffolk Deeds on April 14, 1958, to Lilian Rau, wife of said John

Paul Rau, Senior.

   Third. I hereby nominate and appoint       to be the
Execut    of this my Will and request that   be exempt from
giving a surety or sureties on his bond as such Execut

as he wanted. But the job meant he could be home every night, and the pay was good as well.

With the new year came a new baby, John Paul Rau Jr., born on January 12, 1957. The family was still living in Framingham, and the baby was delivered at Framingham Union Hospital by Dr. Avery at 7:13 p.m. It was one of the coldest nights on record—thirty degrees below zero.

That's me. In about sixty years, I'll tell you this story about my family.

Readville, Hyde Park, and Boston…they were wonderful places to grow up.

Harry Dean was still Mamie's attorney, and he put together all the necessary documents and filings. The bungalow that Jack had built for Mamie was put up for sale, which didn't take very long. James (Jimmy) Mitchell, his wife, Michelle (Mickey), and their young daughter were smart and lucky enough to buy this house that was so well built, with details that were all added by Jack, like the eight-foot-high ceiling in the basement and the granite foundation.

In the early 1970s, when Mr. Dean was in his nineties, he was still a practicing attorney in Boston, walking to Wolcott Square to take the bus daily.

CHAPTER 43

# Meadowview Road

PAUL HIRED A CONTRACTOR HE knew by the last name Skinner to build the house in Readville at a cost of $1,900. In 1958, there were not many houses in this area. Paul was born and raised just around the corner. Lillian was born and raised about a mile away as the crow flies, just the other side of the old racetrack.

The new house was a Cape style, built about 150 feet from Mamie's old house toward the meadow. The front faced the meadow on the road that Mamie had officially named Meadowview Road.

Paul used the driveway that came in by Mamie's house on Colchester Street. It extended down to the new house. That was where he parked the Ford station wagon with the real wood sides. We called it the splinter car.

The Rau's loved the new house, but Paul had plenty to do, as he did not have the upstairs finished and planned to do this himself. Another project that was left for him to clean up was Jack's original house, which sat between Mamie's former house and Paul's new one. Jack had never torn it down because he'd been gradually using lumber from the structure as needed. It was now a rotting mess. Paul's father, Ernie, had a good solution: clear away an area to expose the basement, fill the basement with debris, and then bury the rest with fill.

Over the next year, they burned, disposed of, or buried that entire structure, along with Jack's old screen house by the huge oak tree.

We got a dog about the same time we moved in there. Her name was Moxie. She was a German shepherd–collie mix, and she was a great dog.

While all this demolition was going on, Moxie was digging in under the floor and pulling out big rats. I remember this vividly, along with the glass blocks that had been a wall all taken down and, sadly, smashed.

There was a small wood stove in the old house—the one Jack had picked up in the rail yard. It had come out of a caboose. Jack had used that stove for heat until he moved to the new house. Paul set the stove up in his new cellar near the outside door. Everything was concrete, so it was pretty safe. He supplemented the heat and used it to burn scrap wood when he was working down there. In later years, it wasn't safe with gas and a wood stove to vent into same chimney. My father was now in the oil burner repair business, and he removed the stove.

Down the road, I would resurrect that same stove and use it in my first house in Brockton, though I don't know how I didn't burn that house down. The stove is in my backyard down by the chicken coop today.

The new yard in Readville was huge. The back went all the way to Chester Street, which was actually another house lot. That connected to another lot that went over to the Phillips property. On the right side of the new house was another lot that had been a walkway from Jack's old house out to Forest Street, which was now Meadowview Road.

The area right out in back of our new house had been Jack's main garden area. The soil was amazing and just loaded with worms. Under my mother's clothesline along the fence to the Skeffington's was at one time a big strawberry field. When there was heavy rain in summer the area would be thick with night crawler worms. The Skeffington's had most of Jack's fruit trees—plums, peaches, apples, pears, and even a mulberry tree. That had been his property in the past. Jack had invested a little money and a lifetime of work that helped take care of himself and Mamie to the end.

Mamie was set up in her own room on the first floor, in the front of the house with the bathroom just across the hall. That was the only bathroom for all six of us, but it worked.

She did some of her own cooking—at least breakfast and lunch—and very much enjoyed doing that for herself. She always made the same breakfast: two soft-boiled eggs, wheat toast with butter, and coffee with cream.

Most of her days were spent sitting on a chair she had by the front window where she could watch everything that passed in front of 9 Meadowview Road. Mamie still had that view of Blue Hill out her window that she had been watching for decades.

My room was next to Mamie's in the back. We were the only two who did not sleep upstairs. I spent many a morning, afternoon, and evening with Mamie in her room. She would just talk and tell me stories about what she had done and people she had met or about what Readville and Boston were like during her younger years. There were times that she closed her eyes and just talked aloud of what she was thinking about.

Mamie was very well spoken and quite proper, very deliberate and smart, using words like *glorious* and *grand*, saying "Oh, Johnny, it was a grand structure, and the property was just glorious!"

She was happily reliving the moments, eye's closed and smiling.

She was very religious and did a rosary while listening to Cardinal Cushing celebrate Catholic Mass every morning at nine o'clock, with the door closed. I was not allowed to come in or interrupt.

Except during Mass, her door would be open all day, and I would be in and out regularly.

Mamie had her own television, black and white of course. Nobody had color television yet. The television wasn't used much except for the daily soap operas, which were a new concept; Lawrence Welk on Saturday; Mass on Sunday morning; and Red Sox games.

Mamie loved baseball. She said her favorite player was George Scott. She called him the Boomer and loved to see him hit a "tater," or home run. Then there was Pumpsie Green, another of Mamie's favorites. I sat and watched many a game with her, and later, when I started playing myself, it was fun to tell her about my great plays and hits.

Our whole family ate supper together daily at the kitchen table, and Mamie always ate Sunday and holiday dinners with us. She had her own routine, and I don't remember there being any problems.

My aunts and uncles would come to visit Mamie, and she had friends from her Milton years who were still able to get to the house and visit.

I don't think I ever really knew or understood that Mamie was my grandmother's aunt.

Moxie kept her company as well. She enjoyed that as much as anything. She loved animals. Mamie would just let the dog in and out whenever she wanted, always staying near home.

The house was pretty hectic, with six people and one bathroom, but there were not as many problems as you would think.

Mamie had her routine and didn't deviate very much. The fact is she took great care of herself for many years. It was just normal that she was there.

What none of us ever realized, especially after I started going to school, was that Mamie relished this time alone. It was quiet, and she would stand at the kitchen sink looking out at her old house and yards. Now in her eighties, she had done well for herself and helped her family.

The area still felt very rural in the late 1950s and into 1960. This safe little section of Boston was my childhood playground, a very close and friendly neighborhood. We were the very last street in Boston before you got to Milton. The street dead-ended at a fence where the old Readville Race Track had been in years past.

With the American baby boom in full swing, the Stop & Shop grocery chain began building a warehouse and distribution center in 1955. By 1959 they had built the largest bread-baking plant in New England, capable of producing over seven thousand loaves per hour. The warehouse was strategically located just outside the Readville rail yard, and shipments were coming in on the rail line and leaving on tractor trailers to the supermarkets. The operation ran twenty-four hours a day.

Gradually, more houses went up, and with families having children, the area grew. Technically, Readville went from the Fowl Meadow at the Milton line to just past Saint Anne's Church on Milton Street at East Dedham. It was separated into two sections by the railroad tracks and station. Depending on which side you lived on, the other side of the tracks was "the other side of Readville." This was still all a part of Hyde Park, but Readville did have its own post office, which gave it a feeling of separation. It was like living in a small town, and the post office and firehouse were on "our" side of Readville.

The bus to Cleary Square left from Wolcott Square. You could get to anywhere in the city of Boston for the ten cents that you paid when you got on and a transfer for connecting buses, trolleys, or subway trains.

The dominant religion in Boston was Catholic, and the local parish was Saint Anne's on *the other side of Readville.*

The entire area was as much a melting pot of eccentricities as anywhere in the city. Around the church was strongly Italian. The stores sold Italian goods, and it seemed everyone grew grapes to make wine, but best of all was the bakery. BC Bakery was on Como Road across the street from what used to be Saint Anne's School, which was built and opened back in the early 1960s. I was one of the first students enrolled there for second grade, not the best experience of my life.

The bakery is still there and has been making great bread since back in the early 1900s. We would go in after church, and the smell of fresh dough and baking bread was fantastic. With the twenty-five cents that I didn't put in the collection box, I'd get a big, hot loaf of scali bread with seeds on top, and I would reach in and eat the soft middle while it was steaming hot.

Saint Anne's School was staffed mainly by nuns, and at that time, they all dressed very formally in the black and white robes with their heads covered. Some of them had come from a big convent in Kentucky, and by chance my grandfather's sister-in-law, who was a nun, and was stationed at the same rectory. This did not bode well for me. The third-grade teacher was Sister Rosalita, my nemesis. She had been friends with her, Sister William Theresa, in Kentucky. We'll just say that Sister Rosalita had a thing for dragging me down the hallway to the office by the chubby cheek. She'd hold me by my face, and I would say, "It wasn't me!" Then the sister superior would hit my knuckles with a ruler. They were brutal women to deal with.

Not a word of this went home, as that would have just generated more problems for me, until I was sprung back to public school in 4th grade.

After Jack died, Mamie had so many things to figure out what to do with, but the old steamer trunk full of his woodworking tools went to Paul. That chest sat at the bottom of our cellar stairs for years, and of course I had to see inside. I was like the curious cat.

There were planes of various types and a bit brace with augers, chisels, hand saws, and clamps. I cherished those tools, knowing they'd be mine someday. Until my sister Beth got married in 1965 to Chris Donnelly, another Readville boy. Though I don't know what he did for work before this, I do know he went to work for my cousin Janice's husband doing siding work. My father figured he needed tools to get started in his new trade, so he gave Chris all those tools, telling me that he'd buy me new ones as I got older. He did buy me tools, but there was that other connection with Jack's tools that I had to let go.

There were days I was down in the basement working with tools and banging things on Jack's old anvil. I must have thought the house was sound-proof. There were times Mamie would ask what I was doing, and I'd give the normal answer: "Nothing."

He had tools for doing everything down there, plus my father was a collector of tools as well. But Jack had tools for shoeing a horse and leatherwork, spokeshaves, draw knives. He was a craftsman.

Once I had a power saw and lathe, the noise must have been deafening, but Mamie never said a word. My mother wasn't shy, so if Mamie had said something to her, I would have heard.

CHAPTER 44

# Celebration

BACK IN 1838, READVILLE WAS a remote section of Dedham and a wide plain of land. Many militia companies had been here and were the backbone of protecting the region, and a muster was established and advertised by newspaper and word of mouth. September 11, 1838, would be the day. This date now has other connections to what these men had tried to fight against so many years before.

Here in Readville, thousands of men from all over showed up, and the atmosphere was carnival like. It was advertised that they were here to celebrate.

During the period from the late 1700s through the mid-nineteenth century, these men had come from fighting pirates on the Barbary Coast, some having been prisoners held by the Muslim Beshaw of Tripoli, Tunis, Algiers, and Morocco. For years these pirates tormented the oceans off Africa, taking ships hostage and holding them for ransom. Some men were held for years in horrible conditions with little food, living on dirt floors with no medical care.

George Washington was president while the attacks continued in 1789 when the Constitution of the United States of America was fully in effect. The US Constitution was created on September 17, 1787, and ratified by Congress on June 21, 1788. There were thirty-nine signatures with fifty-five delegates in the Hall of Freedom in Philadelphia, Pennsylvania. New York was the capital at the time.

After the Revolutionary War, the Continental navy was no longer needed and was disbanded. But with the threats and attacks increasing, trade was drastically affected. President Washington established the Naval Act of 1794 to try to bring these attacks under control with the help of the Boston-built frigate nicknamed "Old Ironsides." The USS *Constitution* of the newly established US Navy launched in 1797, the first of six ships commissioned by the Naval Act. Built in the North End of Boston at Edmund Hartt's shipyard, the ship was ironclad and much bigger than other ships of the day. Her first duties were to protect American shipping and ultimately defeat the Barbary pirates.

Now it was time for a celebration that was due them.

But there was a Massachusetts law forbidding selling liquor in containers of less than fifteen gallons. This was to confine sales to taverns and restrict sales in unacceptable public areas. From early in the morning on September 11, there was a tent being frequented by many, and as the crowd grew in size, it formed two lines going into the tent. The tent had a sign with a striped pig clearly visible. Inside was a man who checked patrons' eyes for sties, after which they were given their pint of medicinal optic fluid, which was much less than fifteen gallons. After they'd returned many times that day, the pig would very much look striped.

### The Striped Pig

In the sham of a fight there was a very great slaughter,
And those that survived it could barely get water,
For those that had wells for a quart ax'd a quarter,
Which was a great sight more than they orter.
A doctor who wanted some patients to rob,
Looked in the tent in search of a job,
Disease in the optics he could decree,
For each going in with a sty in his eye.
Next came a sailor under full sail,
Who said he chawed oakum in many a gale,
He gave the porker a boisterous hail,
Then ax'd for a quid of his piggy's tail.
A wealthy distiller next looked in,
To see how they turned grain into gin,
He dryly remarked after drinking his fill,
That was a queer way of the worm on the still.

The sign on the tent was Striped Pig to be seen,
The wonder of Dedham, this four legged thing,
A four penny bit they paid to get in,
Which piggy paid back with his brandy and gin.
The folks at the muster they all agreed,
That this was the pig, for crossing the breed,
For he left his mark for many to heed,
He went in sober and came out striped pig.

The term *chawing oakum* or *picking oakum* sounds odd, like slang, but was common aboard early ships. The rigging on a deep-sea vessel was made of hemp rope covered with tar. When the tar wore out, the rigging needed to be replaced. The existing hemp rope would be cut into pieces a couple of feet long, and sailors would gather on deck to pick the tarry fibers, which became known as *picking oakum*. This was dull and tedious work, hard on the fingers; even though their hands were rough to begin with from hauling rope, this was very tough on the finger joints. Some would resort to using their teeth to work the fibers or *chawing oakum*. They sat and untwisted the hemp rope to individual fibers, and then they twisted the hemp fibers back together. The oakum could then be used for ship caulking; mixed with more tar, it would be forced into openings between the seams of the hull planking by the ship's carpenter, using a *caulking iron*, a tool that resembled a blunt chisel. Then coated in hot tar. This was often part of hard labor and punishment, though not different from forced free work, as sailors well understood.

Camp Meigs was always a special place for the Fourth of July, with ceremonies commemorating the men who trained there and went off to serve during the Civil War. Billy and Murch were the chairmen of the Hamilton Park Association. Later it would be renamed Camp Meigs Memorial Park, and every year, the committee organized an outdoor luncheon for all of Readville. The Bronsdon's always cooked up something special, like a saddle of pork for the 1910 celebration.

When he made the rounds to settle up bills due that might not, we'll say, have been current freight bills, there was always a shop that was slow with money for freight and past due, and that was when Billy shined. Bartering or trading worked much better than cash. He knew that bartering would make him more than he would have charged in cash. But it was a fair trade, with both parties agreeing with a handshake. "We're good?" Billy would ask. There was normally just a nod, and it worked out just fine. A man had to be taken at his word.

The cooking fire with a spit for roasting the pork was set up by the cannons as a central gathering place. Men brought tables and chairs, while others brought food to share as potluck, and there was some wonderful food cooked for the day. The feast started about two o'clock, and everyone enjoyed the day. The children ran and played games, with prizes for the winners. The hoboes or drifters were welcome, and some who had actually participated in the war were duly honored at this commemorating event.

There was a carriage race around the park area every year. The men driving were chosen from a hat like a lottery. It cost twenty-five cents to get your name in the hat, which was part of the game itself. Anywhere from twenty-five to thirty men would be vying for a spot, but only five carriages would be selected for the race. There was a shiny five-dollar gold piece for the winner. Men willing to gamble anted up, and that would pay the five-dollar prize money. Any money left after the day was done went into the fund for maintaining the park's grounds. Billy's hat was used for the drawing, and he always put his and Murch's names in, mainly just to contribute to the draw. They had someone pick the slips and hand them to Billy to read, and if his or Murch's name came up, he would say someone else. Murch, being the money man for the brothers, would make sure he had a nice gold piece for the prize.

One or more of the local taverns would donate a barrel of beer or ale, whichever they had the most of on hand. The committee banned hard liquor until after dark. Ice was brought in great blocks, and someone brought a basket of lemons for lemonade, not a small feat for that time period. There was a big pot of beans and salt pork cooking on a tripod, though Billy always said with a big grin that he liked to put a whole pig's head in for flavor. There was a great display of fireworks at dusk, and a soldier would play "Taps" while the flag was lowered and a cannon fired seven times.

For this tiny area, it was an amazing show of patriotism and love for country.

This was going to be a big night as well. A group of Readville residents were planning to take carriages downtown to watch a great show of fireworks along the newly constructed Charles River dam area. They would be leaving while it was still daylight, but it would be dark coming home. The Bronsdon drivers were used to the roads around Boston in the dark and even more so into Hyde Park and Readville.

Finding a place along the bank of the river, they all set out blankets and were dazzled by the wonderful fireworks show. This was the beginning of many celebrations in and around Boston. There were firecrackers going off all day on the Fourth; they were readily available. There was a factory in Roslindale that was run by Chinese people. It was too crowded in Chinatown to have so much gunpowder.

In 1903, Boston had a male Chinese population of 800. They came looking for a place to live and work. Some had been forcibly brought there from California to break a strike in western Massachusetts. During the late 1800s, Chinese immigration was all but stopped, leaving Boston's Chinatown mostly male with only 18 women. Anti-Chinese sentiment led to the Chinese immigration raid, resulting in the arrest of 234 people and the eventual deportation of many more. By the end of World War II, there were fewer than 2,000 men and 100 women. The land that Chinatown sat on was tidal flats that became tenements for poor immigrants. The Chinese were last and stayed.

Soon after the area called Boston was settled, basically just a spit of land or peninsula there became sections, like Rocksbury. Because it was extremely rocky. Later to be known as Roxbury. The area to the west known as West Roxbury, there was a section of land in between where the railroad crossed at South Street. The area became known as *South Street Crossing*.

Needing a more formal name to have a post office, John Peirce suggesting that the beauty of this land being farms with many hills and dales reminded him of a small town in Scotland *Roslyn* near Edinburg. Then suggesting with its many hills there are dales or valley's creating the name, *Roslindale* and was accepted by the government for the post office. There are areas of Roslindale that are high enough to see downtown Boston.

The design or placement of streets in Boston or lack of design, most were regularly used paths and right of ways added to real estate deals. Many houses were built in places just because someone owned the land and access would be made becoming roads. Driving in Boston with a mish-mash of dead ends and one ways as it was built and populated before there was planning. Modern cities today design streets to run say north and south while avenues go east and west making a grid. The Bronsdon's knew the city of their time to navigate the streets, my father knew every street and back alley when he worked in the oil burner repair business. There was time that particular buildings could be used as landmarks for orientation, but today there are so many buildings that it forms a *canyon* blocking views and sunlight.

# CHAPTER 45

# Growing up Readville

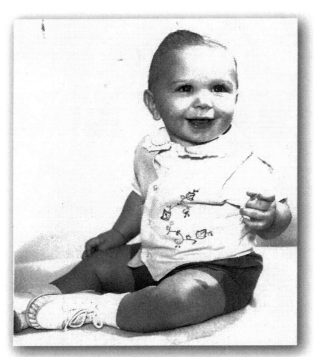

John Paul Rau Jr. 1957

BACK A FEW YEARS, A baby was born on January 12, 1957, John Paul Rau Jr. Me.

I suggested that in about sixty years, I would tell of how I saw *"my Readville."* By now you must know my ancestors and some of their history and stories as well. Remember that back when I started writing my story, I suggested that "without stories we would not have an intelligent reason to wonder who our ancestors were or how they have affected our lives today."

I have a copy of the *Daily Record*, a Boston newspaper, printed on January 12, 1957. Oddly enough, I found it by chance in an old warehouse in Boston, not far from Fenway Park. It was in a pile of old papers. Odd? Or supposed to be there? Who knows. The building was owned by Jerry Ellis, who was one of the Building 19 partners, and the junk in that building reflected the fact, making it even more amazing that I found this newspaper.

Besides being extremely cold the day I was born, an "air bomb slayer" was executed. John Gilbert Graham, from Canon City, Colorado, put a dynamite bomb on a plane, killing his mother and forty-three others, on November 1, 1955. He was put to death in the gas chamber on January 11, 1957. Gina Lollobrigida, Eddie Fisher, and Debbie Reynolds were on the screen. Four rooms of furniture that were regularly $1,195, including everything down to linoleum for the floor, could now be had only $629, and you'd pay just $3 a week.

The world has been in a constant state of change. Fifteen thousand years ago, during the Ice Age, the entire landscape here in New England did not exist as we know it today. As the earth warmed, the glacier retreated, and as the water flowed away to form an ocean, it left small areas called drumlins, an Irish word meaning "little ridge." They would become places like the islands in Boston Harbor today.

I know we talked about this earlier, but now you'll see how this fit into my life as well.

The warming atmosphere even that many years ago melted the glaciers and left fertile land, depositing minerals and soil. Water was left in deep valleys that are now known as kettle ponds like Houghton's Pond at the foot of Blue Hill. There are many small ponds scattered throughout the Blue Hill Reservation and the surrounding area. Ponkapoag is not part of the contiguous Blue Hills and may have been created by the great melting, but it is spring fed, as its native name, "spring fed from soil," implies. We fished these ponds as kids, though I will say we never did very well. I think we just got distracted easily. After all, we were exploring, and everything was new to us.

In the early 1960s, Mr. Skeffington used to take me and Stephen "Skeff" Skeffington out to Moon Island to fish off the bridge that led to the waste treatment plant, until it started backing up and polluting the entire bay and Boston Harbor.

The Blue Hills are another example of land that was hundreds and maybe thousands of feet deep in ice. It was a glacier.

Big Blue was easily seen from Moon Island.

Most houses in Readville were right next to one another, not more than thirty feet apart, but my house and Skeff's were more isolated with woods and open space because of the way Jack had sold lots. He didn't want anyone living very close to his house, at least not while he was alive.

I never met Jack, but I lived and played on his land. It was an amazing place to be, and I say that from experience. There were those little huts we played in, and we found all sorts of old stuff. There was a metal spring mattress in one—no cloth, just springs—an old wood heater, and empty whiskey bottles. Not very long before my father died, I asked him if Jack McDonough drank much whiskey. His reply was a resounding yes! Though I knew this already, it was good conversation, as he liked talking about old times. He was surprised I knew so much.

Skeff was someone I knew very well. I do not remember not knowing him. We played with toy trucks in the dirt behind our houses and grew up together right there on Meadowview Road. We did most everything other kids did and then some. He would be one of our "gang," and we had our territory.

It's funny, as I have a hard time relating to Stephen as anyone but Skeff. Later, others would gain colorful nicknames as well.

Mrs. Skeffington, Theresa, an Italian woman, was the local bookie, calling in numbers for the daily pool. Pick four numbers, and you could bet a dime or a quarter. The results were based on races at the track, and everybody waited for the *Record American* newspaper to come out. The numbers would be on the back page. Winnings were tax free, and they were making big money in the North End of Boston, but that's another story.

Behind Skeff's was an empty lot that was wooded and lower than surrounding properties with big trees for climbing. It connected to a lot that ran over to Mamie's old house. To me, as I remember, it was as big as a football field, but in reality, it was two sixty-foot-by-one-hundred-twenty-foot lots. It was my jungle paradise.

On the other side of our house was another sixty-foot lot that went from Mamie's old house out to Meadowview Road.

To really savor this period I am remembering, you would have to experience the area at the time. I'll do my best to describe this *paradise lost*.

Our street in the early days was almost rural, but with all the amenities of the time. At least my time, which we'll consider to be 1962. The yard was huge. We had natural gas for heat, as did almost everyone, and we had sewerage, electric, and trash and garbage pickup, and street sweepers drove through. We had everything they had downtown. But we had peace and quiet. Parking was nothing to think about. Most neighbors were friendly, and everyone kept neatly trimmed lawns, flower beds, vegetable gardens, fruit trees, ornamental trees, and rows of lilacs.

Watching the movie *Revolutionary Road* brought back memories of 1960s Readville. Leaving doors and windows open at night in the summer was common; nobody had air conditioning yet. Cars in the driveway might have their windows open, and many people left their keys right in the car. Meadowview Road became the place to live. Boston police and firemen moved in, and Readville became their haven.

One house down and across the street was an old friend of my father's, a Readville boy and a Boston cop, Bill Haley. His son Michael would be a lifetime friend, and we had many interesting adventures growing up together.

Grammar school was again the perfect American 1960s-era atmosphere, neighborhood school and all. But this school had history. The Hemenway School on Millstone Road was just a short walk down from Meadowview Road, passing Colchester and Clifford and Hamilton Streets. It was this big brick building. Both my sisters went there, too. We had most of the same teachers as well, another part of the American dream.

Next to the Haley's house were the Domohowski's. Their place had been an empty lot that Jack had given Mamie title to many years before. Now the land she had loved for so long helped pave her future with a home forever.

My grandfather Rau, "Pa"—yup, Ernie Rau—planted a big garden down along the next property line, where one of Jack's driveways used to be. The garden came over toward our house to the old concrete walkway that went up to Jack's original front step, right where Mamie loved to sit on the porch and have supper.

Right next to that granite stepping stone in 1964 was a spot where Pa showed me how to plant one row of green bush beans and beside it a row of yellow wax bush beans. It was all just four feet long and two feet wide, and he told me what to do, and I tended it. We had loads of great beans, and I think that hooked me.

Pa was responsible for my love of gardening. Yes, I believe I do have Jack McDonough's spirit. But with all the time I spent with Pa helping in the Readville gardens and later doing yardwork with him at 105 Brush Hill Road in Milton, I got to stay with Nana and Pa often and at times went with him to his job as the groundskeeper at Milton Academy. He mowed the fields, did all the lines with lime, made sure the grass was watered, and took care of the ice rink.

One day when I was young, seven maybe, I was with Pa at Milton Academy, and my uncle Ernie was with us as well. We were on the ice rink, and Pa was showing how they reglazed the ice with running water from a hose and a squeegee, like cleaning a huge window. At that time, hockey was still just a winter sport, though this being Milton Academy, the ice arena was under a roof. Most ice skating rinks were wide open and had limited use compared to today. After Pa showed what his job consisted of, we all went to another rink somewhere. I saw Pa get to experience seeing an early Zamboni machine for the first time. He was standing next to his boss, "Stokey," and after the machine made a pass and the ice was like glass, Pa turned and said, "Jesus Christ, Stoke." I can still see his excited red face. They had cigarettes to celebrate buying the new machine.

While staying with them in Milton, I would regularly help Pa cook. He did a lot of the cooking, as Nana couldn't stand for long periods. This was fun because I was already practicing at home when nobody was there. See, I did not even consider that Mamie might tell my mother, though I think she must have said something.

Pa helped me try things, in particular cream of mushroom soup. I loved the mushroom flavor. My mother and father wouldn't even think of eating mushrooms. When we went to Nana Anufrom's house, she cooked mushrooms all the time, and my mother always told me that I didn't like them. Nana Anufrom and at least two of my uncles knew how to forage for wild mushrooms; it's becoming a lost art.

Directly across the street from Skeff was the Kontos' house. They were another average 1960s family. Mr. Kontos had been a POW in Japan during World War II, but he seemed OK and was a nice man. He worked for the phone company. They had three boys and two girls. The youngest boy, Jimmy, was my age, and he was another neighborhood friend.

The area from Fowl Meadow was directly behind the Haleys' house. That wilderness ran all the way out to Ponkapoag, and that was our playground during the 1960s. Next to the Haleys were the Giannettis, a large Italian family. Rudy and Steven are lifetime friends. The five of us were the heart of Meadowview Road, at least we thought we were.

We walked many miles before we had bikes, but once we had them, we never thought about anything being very far away, and we went everywhere. Exploring started in the woods behind the houses toward the swamp; that is what Fowl Meadow was known as at the time, *the swamp*, and it could still be. We were not supposed to cross the Stop & Shop warehouse road. Eventually we crossed over the road that went onto the warehouse property, which was actually a private way for trucks and was supposed to be off limits. But it became normal to go across the road and into the meadow and of course to the Neponset River. Once at the river and through the woods along the bank, we came out at Paul's Bridge and an easy way across the river. We gave that river much respect with all the bad things that happen on moving water.

Time has brought me to realize that Mamie had probably been talking to me and telling me stories of days gone by since before I could talk. She likely told me the same stories over the years, and like learning English language at the same age, the more you hear, the more you retain.

There are many that I have finally put to paper here.

I knew our family had deep ties to Readville, and I was lucky enough to have been around many people who were living there. They have been very helpful with my book.

Mamie was seventy-nine when I was born. Many would be happy to get that far in age. She did have a tough life, a bit unusual maybe. But at that time, Mamie still had a much better life than many others: hard work, fresh air, clean living. She did not drink or smoke and was blessed with intelligence. She spoke well, and this was why she was so well liked and respected by many prominent people.

One thing had never occurred to me maybe until now is that I never got to go anywhere with Mamie. She hardly ever left the house. Her priest would come and do a service and communion. I remember the few times a doctor had to see her. That always scared me because I had really never seen Mamie lying down other than that. Standing or sitting in her chair was normal. There were times that Florence Murdock would come to visit. She would park out front, and Mamie went out and sat in her car and talked.

I sat with a friend, Laura, in her studio. She is psychic, and she talked to Mamie. Mamie has always been with me. Laura was also surprised by her stature in that world and that she has pulled many a string for me over the years. Maybe the "four knocks upon my door" was Mamie. With this writing, I did open the door quite literally.

Baseball was Mamie's favorite sport, at least that I knew of at the time. Now I've found out while researching and reading material for this story that she did like football back in her day, as well as basketball. But baseball was good with me. I loved the sport after learning catch and hitting balls in the yard. Now, when I say hitting balls in the yard, that could have been baseball or softball; little Johnny had them all, thanks to Pa. Bats, balls, gloves, hockey sticks, tennis rackets, hockey pucks, basketballs, footballs, volleyballs, all left at Milton Academy by young, wealthy kids after leaving school for the year. He brought them home for me all the time.

I learned to swing those big bats, and by the time I was ten years old, I could swing a bat as big and heavy as Harmon Killebrew's. I would walk up to the field we played on, Meigs, the same camp we learned about in the early history. I'd show up with four or five bats, some baseballs, my glove, and an extra catcher's mitt. Kids were easy to come by, and most knew that we played daily, maybe even three or four games in the summer. We had enough kids for extras on the bench. The city had water fountains with ice-cold water running twenty-four hours a day, and we drank constantly. The water ran through lead pipes I'm sure, but it was always running. There was no Gatorade yet, *it didn't exist*. A tonic cost money and was a real treat. *Tonic* was the term used in

Boston, and I am not sure how far out that goes, but it means any carbonated soft drink. Coke, Pepsi, whatever, is a tonic, so it's "I'll have a tonic."

"What kind?"

"*Coke*"

Down at the flea market in New Jersey about 1967, I asked for a tonic, and the guy tried sending me to a booth selling hair tonic.

Paul's Bridge had a shallow stream running clear and cold into the river. I would stop and drink that water every time I passed, never thinking about pollution.

We would sometimes walk along the stone wall that had been built many years before along the brook all the way up to Blue Hill Parkway or Route 138 today, seeing brook trout and small eels.

Many times, I would come home and tell Mamie where we had gone. Then she would tell me all about the area as she remembered it, suggesting that I stay away from things like the river. Again, she wanted to keep me safe. That was when she'd say, "There are snakes and river rats, so be careful." Those were my two biggest fears, and Mamie probably knew that.

Eventually, finding the old Burma Road just past Paul's Bridge was a great adventure. We walked that road deep into the woods, exploring. Quite a way in, there's an intersection, and going left brought us out to the Hemenway estate, which is actually on Green Street, a very private area. This was probably my first encounter with a property that Mamie had told me about, and even back then at nine or ten years old, I understood some connection. But we didn't come in from Green Street; this was a back way in, and the path coming from the woods opened into a huge, grassy field. I remember it as being like three football fields. This was the front yard, and between the woods and the house was a small pond with shade trees around it. We soon found that there were trout in the pond.

When I say the house across the field, this was not just a house; it was a gothic mansion. Massive and elegant.

Because we were young, we didn't put together where we actually were. The wooded area we came through was thick with vegetation, with the river on one side and muddy, swampy water areas on the other. Burma Road ran between them. Eventually, we found out that if we had gone straight, we

could have gotten all the way down behind the Howard Johnson's just before Route 128 in Canton. We figured that nobody else had ever done this. We used these paths all the time.

Once we knew there were trout in the pond, we started bringing a piece of string and a hook. That was all we needed. Looking under rocks around the area, we found lots of salamanders for bait. We found that as soon the bait hit the water, we would get a bite.

One time about a dozen of us came out of the woods and started fishing. The next thing I knew, someone said, *"A cop is coming,"* and when I looked up, yes, there was a Milton cop about a hundred yards away. I could see his face. My uncle Ernie! The next thing I knew, we turned and ran. Everybody was smart enough to scatter. Michael Haley and I ran down the main path and just turned right directly into the swamp. I think the fear of having Ernie catch me and hand me over to my father overcame my fear of snakes and rats that day. We walked out muddy but safe.

There was another story that there was a huge pumpkin patch in there somewhere. We were determined to find it, but we never did.

Being wetlands, in winter they would freeze for ice skating and hockey. Readville never had a shortage of kids for games, just like baseball. We could have played hockey on patches all over the meadows with extra players. This was the Milton side of the Neponset River. The other side toward Readville was swampy and weedy with tall grass and cattails or cat-o'-nine-tails that were used so commonly by the native people there.

There were small campfires to get warm or heat some hot dogs on sticks. It was great fun outdoors, exercising. What did we know?

The Stop & Shop road became the dividing point between meadow and woods. During the late summer and into the fall, the meadow would be thick with cattails waving in the wind, turning from shades of green to tan, hundreds of acres. There were a few years that the meadows were burned off, basically vandalism or arson—who knows? It seemed to be expected at the time and made for amazing skating come winter. On a clear night with a full moon, you could skate for what felt like a mile safely.

Cattails were a very important plant to the ancient people, and every part of this plant was used. During the Civil War, it was found that the plant could be made into flour, and an area could yield over six thousand pounds per acre.

We learned our way around the swamp over time, feeling as though we owned the entire area from Meadowview Road, the very last street in the city of Boston, out to the swamp. That was our base and safe place, the woods between Meadowview and the swamp. I could literally disappear in those woods, finding perfectly round paths below the thick cane and brush, about three feet in diameter. These ran for what seemed like hundreds of feet well below eye level and were totally camouflaged. It was strategic for when there might be someone chasing or looking for us. We kept them secret; just the few of us knew they were there.

I actually had an MDC cop standing right next to me once. We'd duck and disappear before they got there, and eventually they left, coming back like two hours later looking for their suspect again. Then we'd just wait for them to pull up to us. The classic things we could do would never happen today. We'd immediately say we saw someone out in the swamp about fifteen minutes ago. They'd jump right on the lead and begin to search, and we even helped sometimes, directing them to the spot. Today they'd bring a dog and a helicopter along with channel five.

Saturday morning TV during the 1960s was all cartoons. We had a show in the Boston area called *Rex Trailer* that depicted a western scene and was loved by many. It was real to some of us. The show had an early start depicting Rex and his sidekick, Pablo, in the bunkhouse getting ready. They would be eating beans, cooking them on the wood stove and eating them out of the cans. That was a time when I didn't like beans, so I would open a can of soup or tuna and eat it out of the can.

One Friday, it must have been in 1963, Mike and I had a plan. We got some change by cashing in a few tonic bottles. You got two cents per bottle for deposit return, and they were easy to find. We had already been going up to Wolcott Square with notes to buy cigarettes for our mothers, a common neighborhood practice. Sometimes my mother might have me run up to Mott's, a small grocery store with items similar to Stop & Shop's for twice the price. The store was convenient and friendly; Mott was a fat man with a white butcher's coat, and he knew everyone. There was a meat counter, and he would sell as much or as little as was needed. So if I was sent with a note and money for a pound of hot dogs and there was change, I would buy candy.

Well, on this day we were planning to be up at sunrise Saturday morning and cook breakfast out in the woods, like Rex and Pablo. When we went to Mott's, I asked for two pieces of chicken. Now this was raw chicken, and Mott wanted to see my note. I said I lost it and pointed to what I wanted, and he took it and wrapped it in the white butcher paper. We paid and walked back down to our planned campsite, right behind Mrs. Mogen's house, which was directly across from my house. The idea was to have fire-cooked chicken on sticks like the cowboys. Mikey brought a can of beans and an opener, and I brought a pan with water and some coffee grounds to boil.

When we brought the two chicken breasts back to our camp the night before, we hid them way up in a tree, still wrapped in the paper. Saturday morning, we got our stuff and headed into the still slightly dark woods. We had set up a fire pit the night before and brought matches, a pan, water, and coffee in the morning. When we got there, it was light enough to see that we had been robbed.

The chicken and paper were gone.

At first we figured someone saw us hide it and then stole it from us. Animals or food poisoning never even crossed our minds.

As the sun came up over sleepy Readville, you could hear the sound of birds singing, and you could also hear my mother, maybe two hundred feet away on the other side of the Mogen's house, yelling, "Johnny!"

Just talking about Wolcott Square can make my head spin with things that happened there. You'll remember this was named after former Governor Roger Wolcott, who had such rich history while living in Readville. This is where my side of Readville ended, and it was time to explore in that direction. Its massive granite tunnel was like a gate to the castle, and it was safe there. Leaving Wolcott Square was a stepping stone to learning about Boston in the 1960s. There was really no reason to go that way except for church. We had everything a small town needed: market, variety store with almost everything, package store, luncheonette, barber, gas station, post office…there was more, but you understand.

The one major thing right there was a bus stop for the Massachusetts Transit Authority (MTA, now the MBTA). Get on for ten cents, get transfers, and you were connected to the entire city of Boston and beyond. This held a great future for me.

Summer and no school meant baseball just about daily, and I practiced everywhere. When I hit balls at home in the yard, I would actually hit them across other yards. Then I'd listen for them to either hit something or not. If there was no noise, that was good. When it hit a house, anyone there would disappear.

Playing ball at Meigs was my second home. After swinging the big bats Pa gave me, I was one of the better hitters in Readville.

There was competition.

By the time I was ten years old, I was easily hitting the ball out of Meigs. The teenagers used to come over and make us pitch to them. Once they'd had enough, they would tell me to get up and show them what I could do. They knew I could hit, and I would gladly hit as many balls as they would pitch and try to keep track of where they went.

We had to shag them, though as I told my friends, *If you want to hit 'em, help me find 'em.* The big kids did a lot of swinging, but not much hitting. I was clearing fences, and they would get on me, yelling and chanting names like Ruth and Yaz. But there was one kid, Eddie Coughlin, who got right in my face, said, "Harmon Killebrew," and kept chanting, "Harmon, Harmon…"

Friends still call me Harmon today.

The main person I told about my hitting was Mamie. She made it seem like she waited all day just for this.

Can you just imagine what Mamie must have thought one hot summer day with that big yard, me, and the neighborhood kids? We had all my father's tarps spread out across the grass in my backyard. These were big tarps with water running over them, and everybody was slipping and sliding. There was no hiding this one or the time with all the ladders set up like a roller coaster.

I was intuitive. What can I say?

When I was growing up, my mother never had a driver's license until 1973, so we had to walk or take the bus from Wolcott Square. This was something she had done for years, taking buses, trains, and trolleys all over the city with my aunts, I never saw my father take a bus. Sometimes these trips were fun; others not so much. Expectations were everything, and the promise of food would always help.

There were Jewish delicatessens in Mattapan. Papa Gino's was new in Hyde Park, and I could watch the guy toss pizza in the window. Then heading up Hyde Park Avenue was Ma Riva's, which had sub sandwiches overflowing with real crabmeat. Past the sub shop was Forest Hills and the elevated train to downtown Boston.

When I was eleven years old, I had a good friend in junior high, John Peardon, we went Christmas shopping at Downtown Crossing, getting there by bus and train without any problem. Try that today. His father was a funeral director in Hyde Park and they lived above the business, I saw some interesting things. This was Carroll-Thomas Funeral Home, most funerals I experienced in my life were here.

Mamie knew everyone in the neighborhood by sight. She may never have met many of them, but she knew them by sight. Some, like Bill Haley, a Readville boy, always waved, as did many others, just because they knew she was there.

When I think back, knowing that she was a very smart woman who had experienced a lifetime already, she must not have missed much, at least on Meadowview Road. Having dealt with all sorts of people for so many years and maintaining a sharp mind and good sense of humor. Now that I understand her personality better, I wonder if she smiled if only quietly to herself at my antics.

Now I realize through all the years of many of my ancestors' lives that were influenced by Mary Hickey's life, some may have been touched by Miss Bronsdon or Mary. Others would be driven by the licensed hackney driver, Mary Atchison. After marrying Jack, she was Mary McDonough.

Everyone who was written about in these pages knew Mamie. Not many knew who Mamie really was, just through that window she was perched at for so many years.

For some odd reason, with all the memories and thoughts I have, even about events around their deaths, I draw a complete blank on Mamie's.

So as Laura said to me, "She's right here with you."

I believe.

# EXPERIENCE THE PAST, LIVE IN THE PRESENT

⸻

You've made it to this point after (I hope) reading the contents of my story. It was enjoyable to write this and to remember so many things from the past. With this my ancestors will have some knowledge of their family from the past and how greater Boston has been our home for 350 years. Though it is interesting that Mamie was able to meet and know so many people that were so important to establishing the region. While having the insight to save some information and maybe make her, *timeless*.

## ABOUT THE AUTHOR

READVILLE REALLY WAS AS NICE a place to grow up as a city could be. It helped mold me and many other baby boomers. The public schools in Boston were only as good as what you tried to get out of them. I took the industrial route and became a woodworker. My first woodshop class was in sixth grade. I learned drafting from the time I was twelve years old in junior high school.

Later I traveled out of Hyde Park to go to Dorchester High School. This was a good way to make new friends and expand my world. For three years, I took two buses and a trolley to get there. I still use what I learned there every day, as I am still doing drafting fifty years later. I still enjoy woodworking, though I don't do enough of it these days. My love of gardening runs deep from Jack and my grandfather, Pa. I sometimes wonder if they might be right there watching and enjoying themselves. This has been an enjoyable experience, and now at least this part of me can live on forever.

My title includes the word *ghosts*, which sounds like *paranormal*. I researched the term to see what exactly it refers to, since I wondered if it meant someone typing on my computer keyboard and writing what he or she remembered. Yes, Mamie had a lot to do with this book in the earliest stories, but I am just now realizing that the biggest influence may have been Patrick Henry McDonough. I mentioned his journal in the beginning; I felt he was present while I was writing. I am currently having his 450-page handwritten book filled with poetry and quotes being scanned to let everyone know about him.

Henry can be very persuasive too.

Made in the USA
San Bernardino, CA
09 February 2020